Logical Construction of Programs

Jean Dominique Warnier

Published Under the Auspices of IBI-ICC

VNR VAN NOSTRAND REINHOLD COMPANY
NEW YORK   CINCINNATI   ATLANTA   DALLAS   SAN FRANCISCO
LONDON   TORONTO   MELBOURNE

Van Nostrand Reinhold Company Regional Offices:
New York   Cincinnati   Chicago   Millbrae   Dallas

Van Nostrand Reinhold Company International Offices:
London   Toronto   Melbourne

3° edition
Copyright © 1974 Les Editions d'Organisation, Paris
translated by B.M. FLANAGAN M.A. (Oxon.).
© 1974 H. E. STENFERT KROESE B.V.

Library of Congress Catalog Card Number: 76-25089
ISBN: 0-442-29193-0

Manufactured in the United States of America

Published by Van Nostrand Reinhold Company
450 West 33rd Street, New York, N.Y. 10001

Published simultaneously in Canada by Van Nostrand Reinhold Ltd.

15   14   13   12   11   10   9   8   7   6   5   4   3   2

Library of Congress Cataloging in Publication Data
Warnier, Jean Dominique.
        Logical construction of programs. (L.C.P.).

        Translation of Les procédures de traitement et leurs
données.
        "Published under the auspices of the IBI-ICC."
        1.   Electronic digital computers—Programming.
I.   Title.
QA76.6.W37313.   1976   001.6'42   76-25089
ISBN 0-442-29193-0

TABLE OF CONTENTS

PART I

THE STRUCTURES OF DATA AND PROGRAMS

Table of contents

PART II

THE OPTIMISATION OF PROGRAMS AND THE PROCESSING PHASES

PREFACE TO THE ENGLISH EDITION

With deep satisfaction and confidence I have welcomed this book, on Training for Programming, which is a healthy effort towards the development of a valid methodology for the analysis, solution and documentation of informatics problems and has the additional merit of being based on the explicit concept that Informatics is an autonomous discipline. In this regard I endorse the definition of this discipline as given by the French Academy in 1966: informatics is the science of systematic and rational processing particularly by electronic computers, of information seen as the support of human knowledge and communications, in their economic and social context.

This definition has in fact the merit of emphasizing that informatics is the science of rational processing of information, and that the computer is only a tool, even though it is, at present, the principal tool for the processing of information, and even though the power of that tool has significant consequences.

This problem of definition is not a language controversy: it concerns the concept itself, the very heart of the matter, and in this way, Informatics embodies the computer sciences, but is much more comprehensive and also includes other disciplines, such as the general theory of the information structures.

Informatics, according to that definition and as presented in this book which contributes to its dissemination, is a real far reaching revolution bearing positive consequences. In many cases, the incomprehension or absence of the afore mentioned concepts, is at the origin of the fact that the use of computers has not produced, in practice, results meeting the expectations or the actual possibilities of computers. In these cases, the computer has dimmed Informatics, the tree has hidden the forest. In fact, by placing an excessive emphasis on this or that computer, the general concept of the problem has been put aside.

Taking into account the nature of Informatics intended as an autonomous body whose existence is not necessarily conditioned by that of the computer, this book uses a group of disciplines, such as the sets theory and eloquently shows the difference existing between a problem and the methodologies for its solution, on one side and the final codification of this solution, on the other, the latter being actually dependent of the computer to be used.

By proposing, for programming, a methodology which is independent of the languages which are adopted for it, this book facilitates the communication between the users and the Informatics experts, solving in this way, the increasingly felt problem that arises from the growing complexity and sophistication of computing techniques, that demand a high specialization of the informatics personnel, hindering more and more the communication with non-specialized users.

The theoretical bases used in this book are simple, almost evident, but in spite of this, they had never been considered under this perspective, as systematically occurs with all transcendent things. A programme, after all, is nothing but a virtual mechanism, that completes the electronic circuits of a computer and it is now evident that the methodologies on which programming is based, must necessarily respond, under a mathematical point of view and as proposed by Warnier, to the same concepts that were used for the conception of the circuits which those programmes will complement.

Simultaneously, and taking into account the essence of Informatics, this book proposes that the analysis of a problem and its solution from a theoretical point of view, must be studied independently of the kind of equipment to be employed. It therefore states the principles of economy that will lead to the optimal solutions. The documentation of this solution is also foreseen in the method, which is an invaluable help.

The use of this complex of tools and the resulting documentation permits a quick understanding of the problem under consideration, not only for the person who has done the work, or for other experts in informatics, but also for those users who are not specialized in this discipline.

The structuring into sets of different levels as proposed by Warnier allows also for a clear appreciation of the problem, and as detailed as it may be required. The fact that every sub-set must belong only to one higher level set, permits to establish a number of applications of each of the sub-sets in the higher level sets.

The reasoning expounded in this book leads to a true methodology in Informatics, and without proposing a rigid plan, gives the general outlines for achieving a change in mentality, for both informaticians and users.

In view of the aforegoing considerations, I feel that those of us who are dealing with Informatics or benefiting from it, should be very grateful to the authors for their valuable contribution.

Professor F. A. BERNASCONI
Director of the Intergovernmental Bureau for Informatics
International Computation Centre (IBI–ICC)

The IBI–ICC is an international intergovernmental organisation specialized in informatics which was created under the auspices of UNESCO with which it maintains close ties.

PREFACE TO THE FRENCH EDITION

I am very pleased to present J–D. WARNIER's book for two reasons. First of all, I did not discover the 'method' by myself, but I was more or less pushed by people in the field, that is to say by certain lecturers of informatics in technical institutions who would be far more qualified than I to talk about it here. Secondly, a concern of a pedagogic nature, coupled with a low materialistic desire not to impose a prohibitive price on students for a manual corresponding to instruction left to each teacher's own initiative, made me wish for a small book with no redundance and at a reasonable price.

When, hustled by events, I began to look into the 'method' whose use was growing constantly, I found myself faced with a programming method. However, when my surprise abated, this technique appeared to me so rich that its extension was possible not only in other branches of informatics, such as systematics, but equally in other disciplines such as law, economics, organisation... I did not doubt. This technique for the organisation of thought goes far beyond the programming from which it started. Because of this, it seemed like a minor application of a philosophy; emanating from mathematical set theory, it is such as to be helpful in the organisation or the re-structuring of systems, where this last term is used with its most general meaning.

Moreover, I was conscious that in the ideas of J–D. WARNIER and his team, there could be the beginning not only of the unification of methods for informatic training, but also that of a common language to express thought formulation, and thus I was among those who, despite numerous publications, wished for a small book summarising simply the basic ideas of what I shall not hesitate to call 'the Warnier System'. To my mind, each part should be presented as a whole, a synthesis of the ideas developed in the two volumes already published. I am obliged to J–D. WARNIER for having granted my wish and I am also grateful to him for having taken into account some criticisms, sometimes scarcely justified, that some teachers and I have made.

As it is, this book cannot replace the teacher, even less than the two preceding volumes, but it tends towards being a course summary. The homogeneity of each of the parts is conducive to an especially active form of education, for they are presented as applications of mathematical ideas; in organisation, the laws of program construction are immediately applicable to programming. In accomplishing the integration of the various disciplines, the book thus appears very rich. No one doubts this and that thanks to a few particularly well-chosen examples it renders many services to all those who are concerned with informatics.

As for the casual reader of these lines, even if his immediate preoccupations do not put him in contact with programming (although sooner or later he will be forced to it), may he read this little book without apprehension; I should be very surprised if in the end he feels he has wasted his time.

Jean BOULANGER
Inspecteur Général de l'Instruction Publique

ACKNOWLEDGEMENTS

The production of this book would have been impossible were it not for the industry and active collaboration of many people during its preparation.

Especially, thanks are due to those who gave help in the design and editing notably to:

- Mademoiselle DAMBIELLE, professeur (Toulouse)

- Messieurs BOULANGER, Inspecteur Général de l'Enseignement
      POULAIN, Inspecteur Principal
      BERNARD, Professeur (Lille)
      DASSE, Professeur (Angers)
      HARDOIN, Professeur (Marseille)
      PIOTON, Professeur (Lyon)

Mention must be made too, of the able assistance given by Messieurs DAMBRINE, FLANAGAN, GATEAU and PETIT ingénieurs at CHB who participated in the preparation of the text.

Also of Mesdames FRATI and LEMELLE who were responsible for the typescript and diagrams.

PART I

THE STRUCTURES OF DATA AND PROGRAMS

1— INTRODUCTION

Can programs be designed, coded, debugged and implemented 5 to 10 times faster than is usual? Can programs be written so as to run correctly at the first effective trial? Can program memory occupation and processing time be considerably reduced and, above all, can perfectly clear program documentation be obtained thus reducing maintenance time to a minimum?
The answer to all these questions, from the experience in several hundred companies, in France as in other countries, is 'yes'.

The attempt to apply programming methods already yields appreciable improvements. To-day this effort appears inadequate, since by using the logic of program construction and for the organisation of data that exist, the above-mentioned results may be obtained. The use of this logic presupposes thorough training in theory and in practice.

The aim of the pages that follow is to provide a succinct, but sufficiently complete, presentation of the logic for constructing programs for informaticians, students and other persons concerned with the subject matter under review. Parallel to the development of the tools for data processing, i.e. computers, has appeared a set of techniques generally known as systems analysis, detailed analysis and programming. The reader should be thoroughly familiar with these proven techniques before tackling this book which sets out the logical rules for constructing programs and organising data.

This subject matter has already been elaborated in the 2 volumes entitled: 'Coaching for Programming'. There the progression is deliberately slow; the examples are analysed in detail, the exercises followed by their solutions are numerous. Such an instrument, though necessary for those who aspire to use the logical rules for constructing programs, may not fulfil the need of those who aim to go to the essential and have a comprehensive view of the subject.

The new book which we are bringing out does not replace the existing volumes but completes them. The progression and tempo are very different. The accent here is on the validation of programs, maintenance and the reconstruction of old programs. We refer readers who wish to study the subject in depth and above all to train themselves personally in the use of the rules to the 2 volumes 'COACHING FOR PROGRAMMING'. These publications will allow them to progress from the theoretical knowledge to an initiation into the 'know-how' indispensible to program-designers.
It must also be noted that 'COACHING FOR PROGRAMMING' contains a mathematical introduction which is imperative for those who may not have the required level in this field. Indeed, the language used here is mathematical. Consequently, words such as *relation, mapping, set* must never be used with their usual nor with their informatic connotation but with the meaning defined in set theory. We assume here that the reader is thoroughly familiar with elementary notions of set theory: set, sub-set, element, null set, ordered set, universal set, relation, mapping, set algebra, truth table etc....

The rules under review concern the logic of data processing. In view of this, they are totally independent of the tool used for processing. The increasingly extensive use of computers explains our frequent mention of these machines and of the languages used to program them. In the logical side of this work, the informatician has to organise data whether it be data to be processed, results to be obtained or programs. He has also to write the programs whose logic he has defined and subsequently to amend them whenever necessary. When a program has been written, it has to be debugged on a computer. This stage of the work may well be long and expensive since, if the testing reveals errors, trials have to be re-run until the results are satisfactory. To avoid the expense and delay in the implementation of a program it is necessary to verify it with care before starting the tests. Wide experience has shown that programs constructed logically and rigorously verified, must, logically, run correctly at the first test.

Finally the program must be economical, which supposes:

- a minimum memory occupation
- a short processing time

It is therefore obvious that close adherence to the rules will give the desired results.

The reader may be side-tracked by the apparent simplicity of these rules. He must be warned against the difficulty of their application. They involve a *profound change in the habits of reasoning*. Experienced informaticians should, perhaps more than others, resist deeply ingrained habits. The type of reasoning advocated here will be totally assimilated when appropriate training with outlets on concrete applications has been given for a long period. But when effort and motivation are combined, this extension of the reasoning faculties can be obtained fairly easily. It might be suggested that the type of reasoning used to solve informatic problems at the level at which they are treated here could be applied in many other fields where data or thought is processed. Now, after having researched this limited subject as deeply as possible, we are able to offer another use of this approach with special emphasis on the organisation of data in an information system.

In the following pages, Part I deals with the rules introducing elementary structures for data, programs and results, Part II deals with program optimisation and complex problems in informatics. An exercise (with its solution) appears at the end of each chapter. Those readers wishing to try practical work can thus put their understanding to a test.

2 — HIERARCHICAL ORGANISATION

A program is an ordered set of instructions which process data to provide results.

Programs, like data and results, are information files:

- programs enable data to be processed
- data are the raw material of processing
- results are the produce of processing

When there are long programs, considerable quantities of data, frequent processing runs and urgent needs for results, the computer is the privileged processing tool. When these conditions are not met, man, possibly with the help of accounting machinery is the agent of data processing.

Whatever the means used to process information, the logical construction of data sets and processing procedures is the task of the informatician. This construction could be achieved by approaching the problem with a space-time method, which consists in tackling the problem from the beginning in time. The solution would be sought by imagining the execution of the program in time and writing down the processing steps in space. This approach is not satisfactory, for it leads us to attach equal importance both to details and to essential points; it must be replaced by the hierarchical approach which allows us to go from the set to the element, from the general to the particular.

RULE

Any set of information must be subdivided into sub-sets from the highest level using appropriate criteria for subdivision.
This rule applies to any problem involving the organisation of data, programs or results.

The organisation obtained is independent of the means of processing. It allows us to find an optimal solution.
The example which follows shows how to describe the hierarchical structure of a set of data. The set chosen is a results set.
Example: consider a statistical report of the annual emoluments of the employees of a firm having several plants.

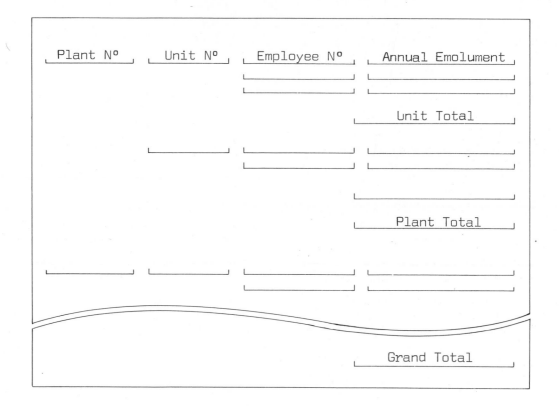

The results on the report can be illustrated as follows:

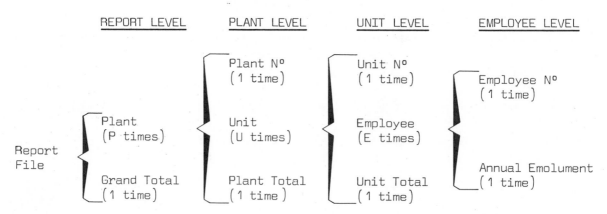

This diagram shows the hierarchical structure of the data contained in the report.

At the highest level, the Report is shown as a set of data. This set is subdivided at the next level into as many sub-sets as there are Plants on the one hand and into a sub-set Grand Total on the other.

We note the number of times that each category of sub-set is present in the set considered as the universal set. The sub-set of data concerning one Plant is repetitive within the 'Report' set and we note (P times), whereas the sub-set Grand Total is present once only.

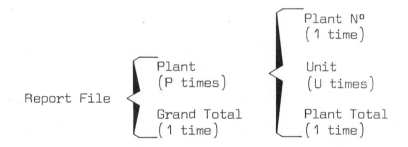

```
                               ┌─ Plant
                               │  (P times )
            Report File  ─┤
                               │  Grand Total
                               └─ ( 1 time)
```

The sub-set 'Plant' is in its turn subdivided. To do this, we can consider the Plant set as universal and we look for its sub-sets. In the data concerning a Plant we always find the Plant (1 time), several sub-sets of data concerning one Unit (U times) then a Plant Total (1 time). The sub-set Unit is repetitive within a Plant.

```
                                                       ┌─ Plant Nº
                                                       │  ( 1 time)
                          ┌─ Plant                     │
                          │  (P times)    ─┤  Unit
         Report File  ─┤                   │  (U times)
                          │  Grand Total   │
                          └─ ( 1 time)     │  Plant Total
                                                       └─ ( 1 time)
```

Now consider the Unit set as universal. In a Unit, we find the Unit N° (1 time), the sub-set of data concerning one Employee (E times) and the Unit Total (1 time).

```
                                       ┌─ Plant Nº        ┌─ Unit Nº
                                       │  ( 1 time)       │  ( 1 time)
                  ┌─ Plant             │                  │
                  │  (P times)  ─┤  Unit        ─┤  Employee
   Report File ─┤                │  (U Times)       │  (E times)
                  │  Grand Total │                  │
                  └─ ( 1 time)   │  Plant Total     │  Unit Total
                                       └─ ( 1 time)       └─ ( 1 time)
```

For each employee there is always the Employee N° and the Annual Emolument. These are elements of the Employee set. There are no repetitive sub-sets in the Employee set.

For each employee there is always the Employee N° and the Annual Emolument. These are elements of the Employee set. There are no repetitive sub-sets in the Employee set.

At the first 3 levels, the subdivision criterion has been to distinguish within a set, those sub-sets that are repetitive from those that are present once only and then, at each level, taking the order of the information in the report into account.

Thus at plant level, we put the Plant N° before the Unit sub-set and the Plant Total after it.
At the employee level, we changed the subdivision criterion since the criterion used for the first 3 levels is no longer applicable. The first criterion can be stated as follows:

• **Subdivide a set if it includes sub-sets that are present a number of times other than once only. (We can also say 'Look for sub-sets'.)**

When we have finished the subdivision using the first criterion, the second criterion is applied to any sub-set which is not sub-divided. It can be expressed as:

• **Write down, in order, the items which make up the set. (We can also say 'Write down the elements'.)**
When we subdivide an information set, it is essential to define the set that is being sub-divided precisely, otherwise the hierarchical approach becomes impossible. To define a set precisely means being able to decide exactly what is an element and what is a sub-set of that set according to its membership criterion.

In the example chosen, once it has been determined that there are several plants in the report, several units in one plant, several employees in one unit, the subdivision does not deal with the Plants (plural), the Units (plural) or the Employees (plural) but deals with the data set concerning ONE Plant (singular), ONE Unit (singular) or ONE Employee (singular).
The hierarchical approach brings to light relations between the sets defined at different levels.

The elements of 2 sets are related by a property. In the set considered, the property is:

An element of a sub-set at a lower level is related to an element of a sub-set at a higher level if the former sub-set is included in the latter.

The direction of the relation is: Sub-set at the lower level towards sub-set at the higher level. The sub-set at the lower level is called the domain, that at the higher level the range.
Consider the sub-sets Plant and Unit in the above example. The Unit sub-set is the domain (D say) and the Plant sub-set is the range (R say). The arrows indicate the relations between the elements.

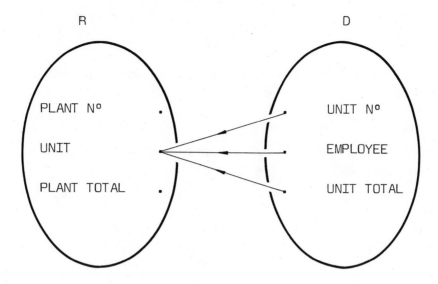

The elements of the range set are called images of those elements of the domain to which they are related. When each element of the domain has exactly one image (no more, no less) we call the relation a mapping.

In the example we have a mapping and if we verify all the relations between the different levels we should see that there is always a mapping in the direction lower level towards higher level.

RULE

In a hierarchical structure there must always be a mapping between each sub-set and all the sub-sets at higher levels.
This rule is a special case of a general law:

LAW

In Informatics any useful relation between 2 information sets must be a mapping.

Whenever this law is violated, the simplicity and clarity of data and procedure organisation is destroyed.

SUMMARY

• *Any set of data must be subdivided into sub-sets starting from the highest level using appropriate criteria for subdivision*

• *The criteria for subdividing a results set are:*

    1. Subdivide a set if it includes sub-sets that are present a number of times other than once only.
    2. Write down, in order, the items that make up the set.

• *In a hierarchical structure there must always be a mapping between each sub-set and all sub-sets at higher levels.*

• *The process of subdividing a set presupposes a precise definition of the universal set currently considered and the knowledge of the appropriate subdivision criteria.*

EXERCISE

Draw the hierarchical results diagram for the computer printed report described below:

Product Nº	Customer Nº	Shipment Nº	Quantity
		Customer Total	
	Customer Nº	Shipment Nº	Quantity
		Customer Total	
		Product Total	

This monthly statistical report shows by product the quantities of each shipment to each customer, the total of all shipments to each customer and the total of all shipments of each product.

SOLUTION

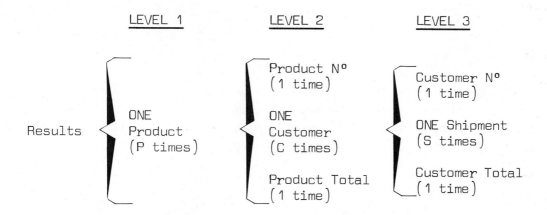

Since there are several rubrics (or elementary data items) the data sub-set ONE shipment can be sub-divided at level 4:

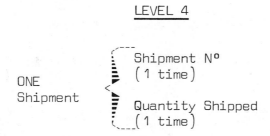

The dotted lines for the braces are used to show that the sub-division is done because of the second criterion.

3 — REPETITIVE STRUCTURES

This chapter shows how to describe the hierarchical structure of the input data of an informatic problem while taking into account results and processing directives. The program is constructed from the input data structure. Finally, as will be seen in the next chapter, the program is validated from the results diagram.

INPUT DATA

The results and the processing required to obtain them influence the input data structure. Thus the output data (results) should be structured before the input data. The input data set, raw material of processing, must be described in a similar way to the results. The data is subdivided starting from the highest level using the following subdivision criterion.

RULE

A set of input data must be subdivided if it includes sub-sets that are utilized a number of times other than once only (criterion 1).

Thus, certain levels of subdivision can be omitted from the data description if they call for no specific processing and provided that other levels are not disturbed.

When the first criterion can no longer be used, the items making up the sub-sets are written down.

Example: take the output file used to obtain the statistical report presented in the preceding chapter. Record layout:

Affiliate N°	Plant N°	Unit N°	Employee N°	Annual Emolument

There is one record for each employee. The file is sorted in the order: Affiliate N°, Plant N°, Unit N°, Employee N°. The sort keys are all numeric and sorted in ascending order.

At the highest level, the file includes a number of data sub-sets concerning each affiliate.

Since there is nothing relating to the affiliates in the report, the affiliate level can be ignored. (We assume that the Plant Numbers are unique.) At the next level, subdivide because there are several Plants.

<u>FILE LEVEL</u>

File { Plant
        (P times)

At this level, the data structure is repetitive: there are several data sets, each relating to one Plant.

Now take ONE Plant as the universal set. This set includes a number of sub-sets, one for each Unit. There are several Units for each Plant (U say).
The following diagram shows the file structure at the first 2 levels of subdivision:

<u>FILE LEVEL</u>   <u>PLANT LEVEL</u>

File { Plant   { Unit
        (P times)   (U times)

At the following level, for ONE Unit, there are several Employees.

<u>FILE LEVEL</u> <u>PLANT LEVEL</u> <u>UNIT LEVEL</u>

File { Plant   { Unit   { Employee
        (P times)   (U times)   (E times)

For each employee, all the items are present once only. The diagram is completed by writing down the items for an Employee.

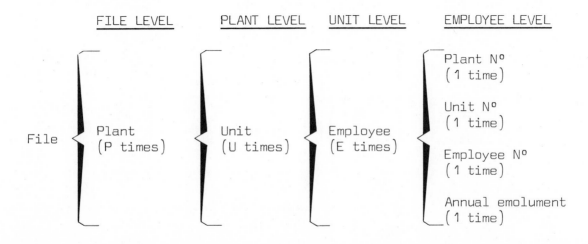

<u>FILE LEVEL</u> <u>PLANT LEVEL</u> <u>UNIT LEVEL</u> <u>EMPLOYEE LEVEL</u>

File { Plant   { Unit   { Employee   { Plant N°
        (P times)   (U times)   (E times)   (1 time)

                                                    Unit N°
                                                    (1 time)

                                                    Employee N°
                                                    (1 time)

                                                    Annual emolument
                                                    (1 time)

In this example, the data structure is said to be repetitive at the File, Plant and Unit levels.

An input data set of repetitive structure is a set in which several sub-sets of the same type are utilized.

THE PROGRAM

RULE

The hierarchical structure of the program is deduced from that of the input data.

RULE

• If an input data sub-set is of repetitive structure, so is the corresponding program sub-set.

RULE

A program of repetitive structure always includes a repetitive sub-set preceded by a sub-set 'begin' to be executed 1 time and followed by a sub-set 'end' to be executed 1 time within the set.

Example: The program which processes the data described above to obtain the results presented in the preceding chapter.
Here are the diagrams for the data and results which have already been constructed:

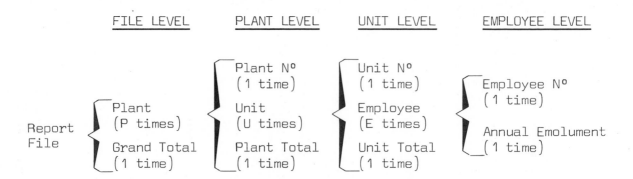

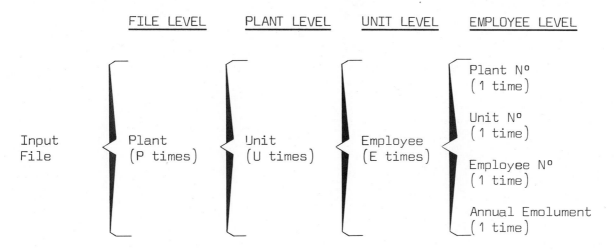

By applying the rules outlined above, the program deduced is made up of a nested repetitive structure.

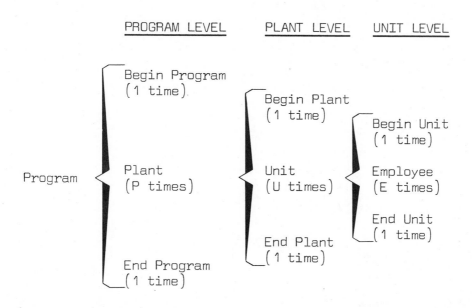

The diagram illustrates the hierarchical structure of the program whose logic is thus wholly determined. It is possible to translate the diagram into another which represents the space-time operation of the program, i.e. the flowchart:

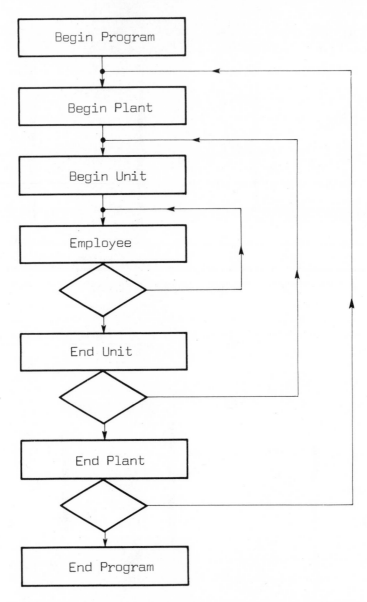

Each sub-set corresponding to a rectangular symbol in the flowchart is called a *logical sequence*.

A logical sequence is a sub-set of program instructions that are all executed the same number of times at the same place in the program; i.e. under the same conditions.

As a consequence, 2 logical sequences are mandatorily separated by a junction or by a branch instruction. Inversely, 2 junctions or branch instructions are always separated by a logical sequence.

A logical sequence is a set. It can contain 0,1 or several (N) instructions. A logical sequence that contains no instructions is a null sequence. In this case, it need only be mentioned in the program documentation.

In this example, all the program sub-sets are of repetitive structure and correspond to repetitive sub-sets in the data file. The function of a repetitive program set is to assure all the processing that is common to a data set (begin and end processing sub-sets) in conjunction with the processing of each data sub-set (repetitive processing sub-set). For example, the Plant set in the program is of repetitive structure thus the begin Plant sub-set contains instructions concerning the Plant N°, the end Plant sub-set contains instructions concerning the Plant total and the repetitive Unit sub-set contains instructions concerning the Units within one Plant.

Whereas the repetitive sub-set is programmed once but is *executed* N times, the data sub-set processed is *used* N times.

RULE

The same data sub-set can be used several times during the execution of a particular program; this is the case of tables or of certain codes. This sub-set although present once only, is described as though it were present N times during the running of the program.

The notation N times for an input data set means that the set is utilized N times. The same notation for a program set means that, although present only 1 time in the program file, the set is executed N times.

Example: Take a sequential file of Orders, sorted in ascending order on the Order N° and containing one record for each product ordered. An Order can contain several products.

Order N°	Product N°	Quantity

The tariff file giving the unit price for each Product has been recorded beforehand in core memory. It is sorted by Product N° and contains one record for each product.

Product N°	Unit Price

Each product can be valued by searching the tariff sequentially. The error 'unit price missing' is excluded.

The report valued by products must be in the same order as in the Order file, which prevents our regrouping the different valuations for the same product.

Report model:

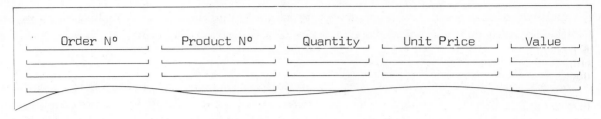

Here is the diagram for the results.

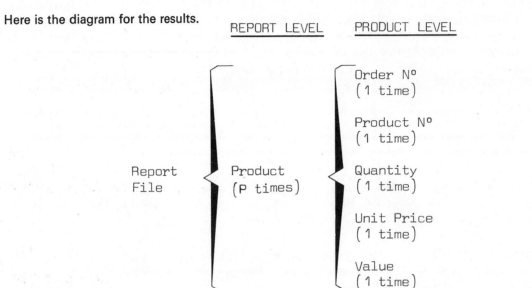

Note that there is no output common to the sub-set of an Order. Therefore the Order level is not de-scribed in the input data structure, because it does not disturb other levels.

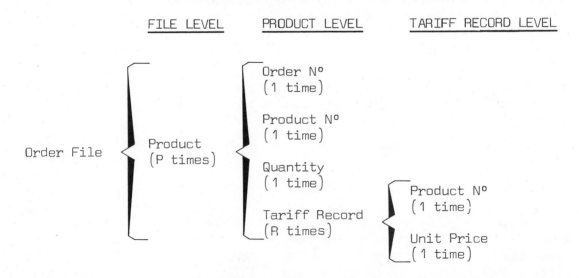

The tariff, although present 1 time, is consulted P times (1 time per Product). Each consultation involves the inspection of R records of the tariff to find the unit price for one particular product.

As a result of applying the rules given above, the input data structure:

- ignores the Order level
- considers the tariff as present P times (as many times as there are products).

The program structure is deduced by using the construction rule already given: If an input data sub-set is of repetitive structure so is the corresponding program sub-set.

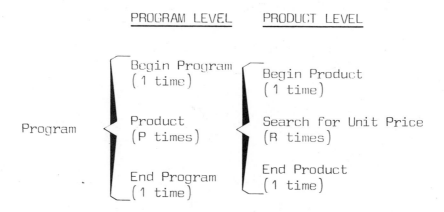

The product data records are used repetitively, but although each record has the same format, the contents are different. In the case of the tariff file, considered as a whole, it is utilized as many times as there are products to value. There is, however, only one tariff file since here, not only is the format the same for each utilisation but the contents too. Thus the tariff file is described as a sub-set of the product data set since it is used, as a whole, as many times as there are product records.
Here is the flowchart of the sequences for this problem:

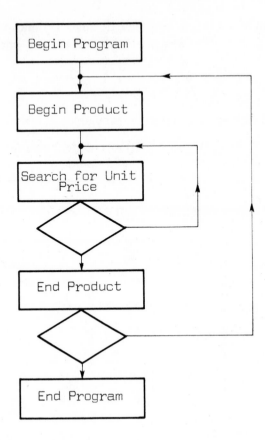

We have been studying the organisation into logical sequences of a program made up of nested repetitive structures. Before continuing with the next part of organisation into logical sequences, we shall study, in the next chapter, detailed organisation. This will allow us to see more precisely what a program is.

SUMMARY

• *Input data, the raw material of processing performed during the execution of the program, must be organised into hierarchical sub-sets taking into account the results and processing directives.*

• *The criteria for subdividing an input data set are:*
    1. Subdivide a set if it includes sub-sets that are utilized a number of times other than once only.
    2. Write down in order the items that make up the set.

• *The hierarchical structure of the program is deduced from that of the input data.*

- *If an input data sub-set is of repetitive structure so is the corresponding program sub-set.*

- *The program is an ordered set of instructions and can be redefined as an ordered set of logical sequences where a logical sequence is a sub-set of instructions executed the same number of times at the same place in the program.*

- *A program of repetitive structure always includes a repetitive sub-set preceded by a sub-set begin to be executed 1 time and followed by a sub-set end to be executed 1 time within the set.*

- *The last instruction of the repetitive sub-set must be a conditional branch instruction.*

- *Diagram and flowchart of a simple repetitive structure of a program P to process a set of data which includes N sub-sets.*

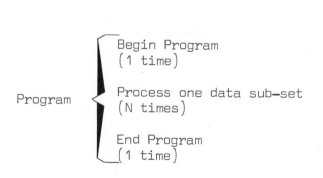

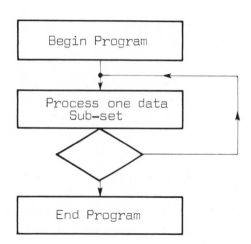

- *The organisation of a program is done in 2 stages:*

  - *organisation into logical sequences*
  - *detailed organisation (instructions)*

EXERCISE

Monthly statistics of emoluments are required by affiliate and within each affiliate by plant.
Report Layout:

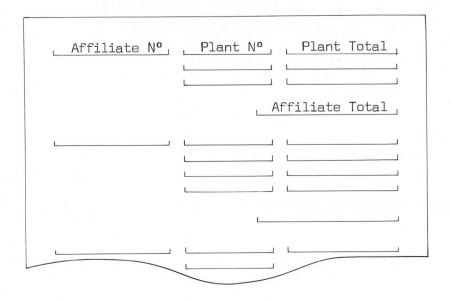

Input data: (sorted by Affiliate N°, Plant N° and Unit N°) one record per Employee:

Affiliate N°	Plant N°	Unit N°	Employee N°	Amount

CALCULATIONS

- Accumulate amounts paid to each employee giving the plant total
- Accumulate plant totals giving the affiliate total

SOLUTION

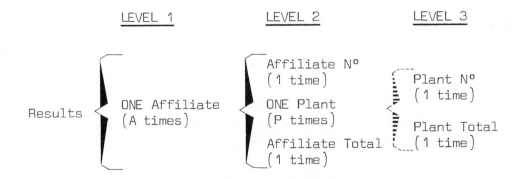

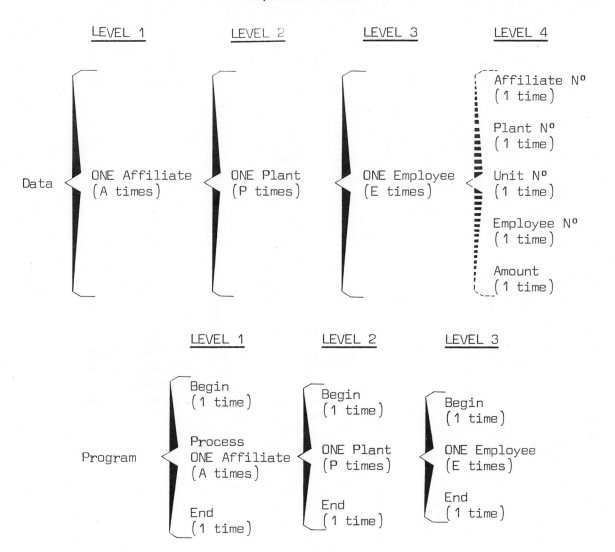

LEVEL 1   LEVEL 2   LEVEL 3   LEVEL 4

Affiliate Nº
(1 time)

Plant Nº
(1 time)

Data   ONE Affiliate   ONE Plant   ONE Employee   Unit Nº
        (A times)   (P times)   (E times)   (1 time)

Employee Nº
(1 time)

Amount
(1 time)

LEVEL 1   LEVEL 2   LEVEL 3

Begin   Begin   Begin
(1 time)   (1 time)   (1 time)

Program   Process   ONE Plant   ONE Employee
           ONE Affiliate   (P times)   (E times)
           (A times)

End   End   End
(1 time)   (1 time)   (1 time)

Flowchart of the logical sequences:

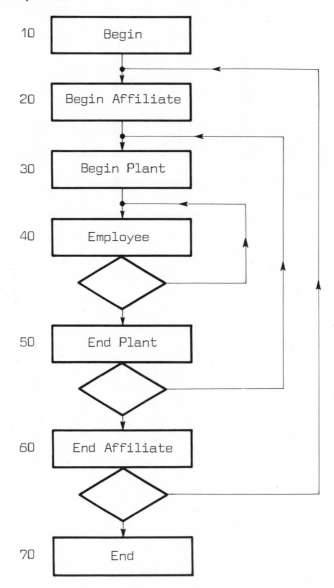

4 — DETAILED ORGANISATION OF A PROGRAM

GENERAL

The organisation of a program is done in 2 stages:

- organisation into logical sequences
- organisation into an ordered set of instructions

The first stage has been studied; the second is necessary for coding the program in the appropriate language: Cobol, Fortran, Basic, assembler etc. . . .

For the detailed organisation, the sequences must be numbered and lists of instructions by type must be drawn up:

- **input (read) instructions**
- **branch and preparation of branch instructions**
- **calculations and preparation of calculations instructions**
- **output and preparation of output instructions**
- **subroutine call instructions.**

The relation between each sub-set of instructions and the set of logical sequences is then studied. The relation is defined by the property:

An instruction is related to a sequence (element of the set of logical sequences) if it is executed the same number of times at the same place of the program.

If an instruction is related to several logical sequences, it must be programmed several times: once in each sequence. Thus the mapping between the instruction set (domain) and the logical sequence set (range) is validated.

If a group of instructions is related to several logical sequences, it should be made into a sub-routine. The sub-routine is constructed and programmed once only and is called as many times as there are sequences in which it should be executed. The case of sub-routines in a program is analogous to that of tables in input data sets: physically present once only, these subsets are called several times at different instants of time.

The detailed organisation is terminated by merging the lists of instructions by type into one complete list of instructions, sorted, sequence by sequence, into the order in which they should be executed. Here, as an example, is the detailed organisation of the program of annual emoluments studied in the preceding chapter.

Example: the starting point is the flowchart of logical sequences to which the sequence numbers have been added. The numbering is 10 by 10 to leave gaps to add sequences for later program amendments.

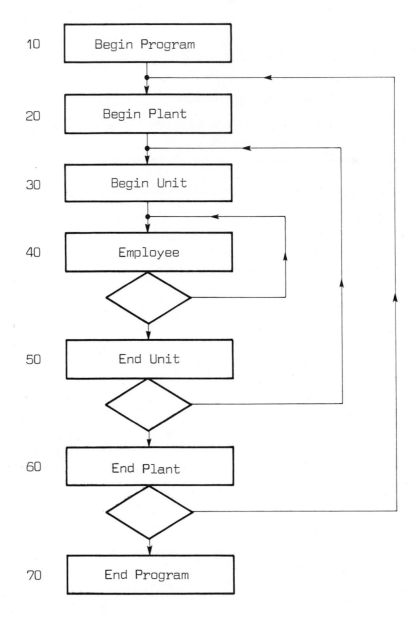

INPUT (read) INSTRUCTIONS

First, write down the list of input instructions. Here, initially, this list contains one element only since there is only one physical input file. The instruction is READ A RECORD FROM THE FILE (READ

FILE). The answer to the questions *'how many times?'* and *'when?'* do we have to read a record is, in the case of standard sequential files: 'As many times as there are records in the file plus one'. Indeed, the end of file record must also be read when the file is sequential.

Where is the sequence executed as many times as there are employees plus one? There is no such sequence, but there is a sequence executed as many times as there are employees: sequence N° 40, and a sequence executed 1 time in the program at the beginning: sequence N° 10. Thus, as many reads can be executed as there are employees plus one.

To ensure the correct allocation of the input instructions, it suffices to execute 1 read in sequence N° 10 and another in sequence N° 40. The problem of the input instructions has been solved by using 2 instructions for the same file:

- one in sequence 10: read the first record of the file
- another in sequence 40: read another record of the file or the end-of-file record.

BRANCH INSTRUCTIONS

Secondly write down the list of branch instructions. This is easy, since each branch instruction is identified on the flowchart by the diamonds attached to the rectangles of the logical sequences.

Note that the diamond is attached to the rectangle to show clearly that the branch instruction is the last element of the sequence. Indeed, the branch is executed the same number of times as the sequence that it terminates.

In a repetitive program set, there is exactly one branch instruction. This instruction is always in the same place: it is the last instruction of the repetitive sub-set.

Example: in the problem under review, the branches are listed by reading the flowchart and noting their conditions:

Sequence	Instruction	Next sequence
• 40 —	if identifier of Unit read = identifier of Unit processed	40
• 50 —	if identifier of Plant read = identifier of Plant processed	30
• 60 —	if NOT end of file ($\overline{EOF}$)	20

The list must be completed by adding the preparation of branch instructions.

PREPARATION OF BRANCH INSTRUCTIONS

To perform a branch instruction, it must be determined whether or not the data made available by a read instruction belongs to the set indicated for a certain processing.

Example: using the same example, an employee record must be processed immediately if its Unit N°

and Plant N° are the same as the Unit N° and Plant N° being processed. If not, it belongs to the next Unit. Thus end Unit processing for the current unit and begin Unit processing for the next unit must be executed before dealing with the Employee processing.

A branch instruction depends on a comparison. The comparison requires 2 terms which must both be available:

- the reference criterion which is in core memory
- the identification criterion which is in the record read

The identification criterion accompanies the data sub-set to be identified. The reference criterion must be kept in core memory as long as is necessary to process the data sub-set concerned.

The function of preparation of branch instructions is to make these criteria available when they are not automatically present.
The list of preparation of branches is compiled by going through the list of branch instructions already completed. For each instruction, ask the question 'are the 2 criteria present?' If one is absent, the instruction required to make it available is determined and then the mapping between these instructions and the logical sequences is validated by using the general rule indicated for other types of instruction.

Example: here is an application of these rules in the example under review: The branch at the end of sequence 40 is conditioned by the comparison of the identifier of the Unit read (identification criterion) with the identifier of the Unit processed (reference criterion). If the Unit N° processed is not saved, the comparison is impossible. So the following instruction is programmed:

Transfer Unit N° read to Reference Unit N° field.

The *Unit N°* must not be confused with the *identifier of a Unit*. In the example, the number of the last Unit of a Plant could be the same as the number of the first Unit of the next Plant, thus to change Units correctly, the Plant N° must be integrated into the identifier of the Unit and the comparison must be done on the two numbers together.

For the branch instruction at the end of sequence 50, the reference criterion is also missing: the Plant N°. On the other hand, the end of file is no problem.
The Plant N° must be stored as many times as there are Plants and at the beginning of each Plant, i.e. in sequence 20.

The Unit N° must be stored as many times as there are Units and in the beginning of each Unit, i.e. in sequence 30.

Here is the list of the instructions required to prepare the branches:

Sequence	Instruction

- 20 — Transfer the Plant N° to reference Plant N° field
- 30 — Transfer the Unit N° to reference Unit N° field

The following rule should be remembered in connexion with the preparation of branch instructions.

RULE

The processing of a data set must be preceded by the transfer into core memory of the reference criterion of this set.

CALCULATIONS

In the example, the list of calculations is easy to draw up. The totals of the annual emoluments have to be obtained by unit, and by plant. A grand total for the whole enterprise must appear at the end of report. For each type of accumulation, fields must be cleared.

The relation between the instructions and the sequences is always the same. Here is the list of the calculations and their preparation:

- 10 — Clear Grand Total
- 20 — Clear Plant Total
- 30 — Clear Unit Total
- 40 — Add Annual emolument to Unit Total
- 50 — Add Unit Total to Plant Total
- 60 — Add Plant Total to Grand Total

OUTPUT INSTRUCTIONS

To complete this example, there remain only the editing and output instructions. Each output instruction is followed by a restoration of the output field.

If the various elements of a line must be transferred to the output area under different conditions then the editing of the elements should be detailed. Here, adhering to the same relation for the mapping, is the list of the editing instructions and the outputs:

- 20 — Edit Plant N°
- 30 — Edit Unit N°
- 40 — Edit Employee N°
- 40 — Output and restore print line
- 50 — Edit Unit Total
- 50 — Output and restore print line
- 60 — Edit Plant Total
- 60 — Output and restore print line
- 70 — Edit Grand Total
- 70 — Output and restore print line

The instructions are now all allocated to the sequences. What remains is to compile the list of the sequences after having sorted the instructions in each sequence. On completion, all the fields of core memory for the program are defined and thus the memory layout is prepared: input areas, reference fields, calculation fields and output areas.

DETAILED INSTRUCTION LIST

From the 4 lists obtained (5 if there were any sub-routine calls), which have been reproduced on the left of the page, the detailed instruction list can be drawn up for coding the program in the appropriate language. This list is written, sequence by sequence, in ascending order of the sequence numbers.

Within a sequence, the order of the instructions is usually the following:

- preparation of branches
- preparation of calculations and calculations
- preparation of output and outputs
- inputs
- branches

Recapitulation of Lists already obtained

10 — Read 1st Record
40 — Read another Record or EoF 𝔄

40 — If iden. Unit = ident. Ref. Unit 40
50 — If ident. Plant = iden. Ref. Plant 30
60 — If $\overline{\overline{EOF}}$ 20

20 — Transfer Plant N° read to Ref plant N°
30 — Transfer Unit N° read to Ref Unit N°

10 — Clear Grand Total
20 — Clear Plant Total
30 — Clear Unit Total
40 — Add Annual Emolu. to Unit total
50 — Add Unit total to Plant total
60 — Add Plant total to Grand total

20 — Edit Plant N°
30 — Edit Unit N°
40 — Edit Employee N°
40 — Output and restore Print line
50 — Edit Unit total
50 — Output and restore Print line
60 — Edit Plant total
60 — Output and restore Print line
70 — Edit Grand Total
70 — Output and restore print line

Sorted List of the instructions of the program

10 — Clear Grand Total
 Read 1st Record
20 — Transfer Plant N° to Ref Plant N°
 Clear Plant total
 Edit Plant N°
30 — Transfer Unit N° to Ref Unit N°
 Clear Unit total
 Edit Unit N°
40 — Add Annual Emol. to Unit total
 Edit Employee N°
 Output and restore print line
 Read another record or $\overline{\overline{EOF}}$
 If ident. Unit = ident. Ref. Unit 40
50 — Add Unit total Plant total
 Edit Unit Total
 Output and restore print line
 If ident. Plant = ident. ref. Plant 30
60 — Add Plant total to Grand Total
 Edit Plant total
 Output and Restore print line
 If $\overline{\overline{EOF}}$ 20
70 — Edit Grand Total
 Output and Restore Print line

Note sequence 40 in this example. This sequence begins with a calculation, then there is an output. At the end of the sequence the following records is made available by an input instruction, then it is tested by a branch-instruction.

The program is now completely determined. There is not a single instruction in the preceding detailed list that is dependent upon a particular type of computer. The solution just described can easily be translated into any language for any machine.

VALIDATION OF A PROGRAM BY USING THE OUTPUTS

A program must be validated before being sent for debugging on a machine. In this way satisfactory results can be obtained at the first trial.

The diagram of the output file is used to validate the program.

There are the following possibilities of errors in logic in a program:

- **output of an item of information that should not be in the results,**
- **absence of an item of information that should be in the result,**
- **repetitive output of an item that should appear once only,**
- **random output of an item that should appear only under certain conditions.**

To eliminate such errors as these, a certain number of controls should be performed. The main one is to verify that each output is programmed in the right sequence.

The first step in the control is carried out when the program has been subdivided into logical sequences. This diagram is compared with that of the outputs; for each item output there must be a logical sequence executed the required number of times at the appropriate place in the program.
The second step in the control is carried out when the detailed organisation is completed. The diagram of the outputs is compared with the detailed list of the instructions of the program.

Example: In the emoluments statistics problem, here are the diagrams of the program and output:

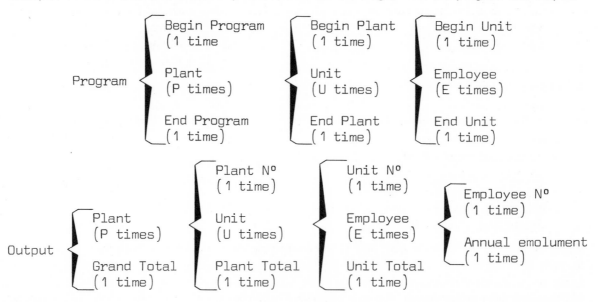

The plant N° must be edited once per plant at the beginning of each plant: the sequence 'Begin Plant' is there for that to be done. The unit N° must be edited once per Unit: this can be done in the sequence Begin Plant. All the unsubdivided sub-sets or items from the output diagram should thus be reviewed: Employee N°, Annual Emolument, Unit Total, Plant Total and Grand Total.
The second step is performed in the same way. Starting from the output file and the final detailed list the same verifications are made in order to detect transcription errors that can occur when the list is written out.
After the controls, the test sample must be made up. This should allow all the sequences of the

program to be executed and those that are repetitive at least twice. Coding errors are difficult to eliminate completely. On the other hand, errors in logic must be totally eliminated. Experience has shown that this is possible by using the rules that we have started to outline here.

SUMMARY

- *The detailed organisation of a program is accomplished by drawing up lists of instructions by type in the order:*

  - *Inputs (read)*
  - *Branches*
  - *Preparation of branches*
  - *Preparation of calculations and calculations*
  - *Preparation of outputs and outputs*
  - *Sub-routine calls*

- *The mapping of the instruction sets into the set of logical sequences must be validated. An instruction is related to a sequence if it is executed the same number of times at the same place in the program. Then, the detailed list must be drawn up by merging the previous lists by type and sorting the instructions within the sequences.*

- *Given a data set to process, the usual order of the instructions in the corresponding sequence is:*

  - *Preparation of branches*
  - *Preparation of calculations and calculations*
  - *Preparation of outputs and outputs*
  - *Inputs (read)*
  - *Branches.*

- *The locations of the sub-routine calls depend on the function of these routines.*

- *The starting point for program validation is the output diagram. Each output must be programmed in the appropriate sequence.*

EXERCISE

Carry out the detailed organisation of the exercise at the end of chapter 1.3. Don't forget to use the results to verify the solution. Here are the results diagram and flowchart:

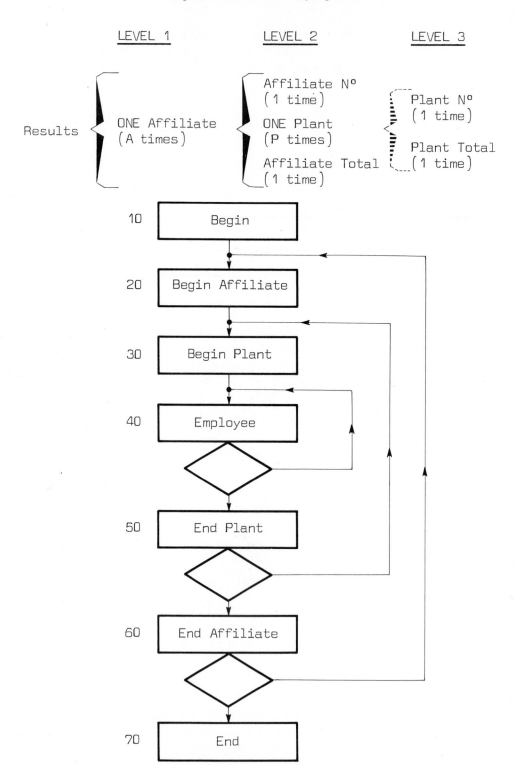

SOLUTION

Instruction Lists by Type:

Read

- 10 Read 1st record
- 40 Read

Branches

- 40 If Plant Ident. = Ref. Plant Ident.   40
- 50 If Affiliate Ident. = Ref. Affiliate Ident.   30
- 60 If $\overline{EOF}$ 20

Preparation of Branches

- 20 Transfer Affiliate N° to Ref. Affiliate
- 30 Transfer Plant N° to Ref. Plant

Calculations

- 20 Clear Affiliate total
- 30 Clear Plant total
- 40 Add Amount to Plant total
- 50 Add Plant total to Affiliate total

Outputs

- 20 Edit Affiliate N°
- 30 Edit Plant N°
- 50 Edit Plant total
- 50 Print and restore
- 60 Edit Affiliate total
- 60 Print and restore

Sorted Instruction List

- 10 Read 1st record

- 20 Transfer Affiliate N° to Ref. Affiliate

  Clear Affiliate total

  Edit Affiliate N°

- 30 Transfer Plant N° to Ref. Plant

  Clear Plant total

  Edit Plant N°

- 40 Add Amount to Plant total

  Read

  If Plant Ident. = Ref. Plant Ident.   40

- 50 Add Plant total to Affiliate total

  Edit Plant total

  Print and Restore

  If Affiliate Ident. = Ref. Affiliate Ident.   30

- 60 Edit Affiliate total

  Print and Restore

  If $\overline{\overline{EOF}}$ 20

5 — ALTERNATIVE STRUCTURES

Up to now the structure of data, program and results sets studied has always been repetitive, i.e. at a given level, the set considered as universal was subdivided:

- in the case of a data set, into sub-sets of the same kind present or utilized several times within the set,
- in the case of a program set, into one sub-set to be executed several times within the set preceded by a sub-set 'begin' and followed by a sub-set 'end' both to be executed once only.

In this chapter it will be shown that there is one and only one other elementary structure: the alternative structure.

A data set of alternative structure is a set within which there are one or many sub-sets whose presence or utilization is random. If there are several, they are mutually exclusive.

A program set of alternative structure is a set which includes two or more mutually exclusive sub-sets whose execution is random and the sub-sets begin and end to be executed once within the set.

In the diagram for output data sets the random PRESENCE of a sub-set is noted: 'O or 1 times'.

In the diagram for program sets, the sub-sets or logical sequences whose EXECUTION is random are noted: 'O or 1 times'.

The number of times noted on the diagram always indicates:

- **for a data set, the number of times the sub-set is present in case of an output data set, or utilized in case of an input data set,**
- **for a program set, the number of times the sub-set is to be executed.**

OUTPUT DATA

An information set of alternative structure includes at least one sub-set present 0 or 1 times. When several sub-sets are present 0 or 1 times within a set, they must be mutually exclusive for the structure to be alternative.

Example: a list of statements of accounts.

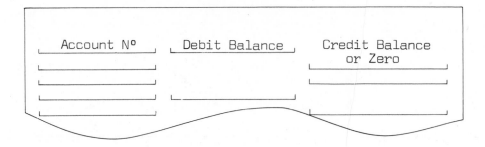

Here is the diagram showing the hierarchical structure of this list:

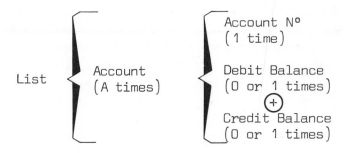

The symbol ⊕ (non-inclusive or) is used to indicate that, for an account, the balance must be either Debit or Credit but cannot be both.

When there is only one sub-set present 0 or 1 times in a results set, the set structure is alternative. The second term of the alternative (complement of the sub-set) corresponds to an absence of processing.

Example: Some, but not all, of the employees of an enterprise have the right to an end of year bonus whose amount is shown in a report.

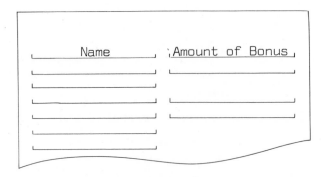

The diagram of the hierarchical structure of this report is:

$$\text{Report} \left\{ \begin{array}{l} \text{Employee} \\ \text{(E times)} \end{array} \right. \left\{ \begin{array}{l} \text{Name} \\ \text{(1 time)} \\ \\ \text{Amount of bonus} \\ \text{(0 or 1 times)} \end{array} \right.$$

INPUT DATA

Up to now, data sets have been considered as regards their structure but not as regards their contents.

The value of a code appears in the hierarchical structure of the input data when it must be tested during the execution of the program. For example, a code used 1 time in a data set can take the value x or some other value ($\bar{x}$). This value is to be tested by the program. The set is described as follows:

$$\text{Set} \left\{ \begin{array}{l} \text{Code} \ [\text{x, 0 or 1 times}] \end{array} \right.$$

which means: in the set the code is always utilized 1 time but it has the value x, 0 or 1 times and the value $\bar{x}$ (some other value) 0 or 1 times.

In an input data set, there is another case of an alternative structure: in the set a sub-set is physically present 0 or 1 times.

Example: take a file, processed monthly, which may or may not contain data depending on the month. The diagram will be:

$$\text{Input Data} \left\{ \begin{array}{l} \text{File} \\ \text{(0 or 1 times)} \end{array} \right.$$

Thus, there are two kinds of alternatives in input data sets:
- **the alternative concerning the physical presence of a sub-set used,**
- **the alternative concerning the value of the contents of a field to be tested.**

THE PROGRAM

The rule given in the preceding chapter, which says that the program structure is deduced from that of the input data, remains valid when the data set includes alternatives.

RULE

If the input data set is of alternative structure, so is the corresponding program set.

RULE

A program set of alternative structure always includes two or more mutually exclusive sub-sets each executed 0 or 1 times. These sub-sets must be preceded by a sub-set 'begin' and followed by a sub-set 'end' each to be executed 1 time in the set.

Take a sub-set A utilized 0 or 1 times in a set of input data D. The program set to process D includes four sub-sets:
- 'begin D' which is terminated by the test for the utilization of A,
- 2 sub-sets, one of which is null, each to be executed 0 or 1 times within the set: 'process A' and 'not A',
- finally the sub-set 'end D' which is to be executed 1 time within the set.

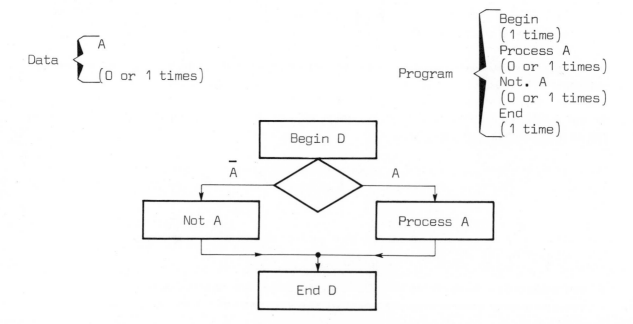

As has been said earlier, the notation 0 or 1 times means that the set A of input data is used 0 or 1 times within the data set and that the set which processes A is to be executed 0 or 1 times within the program set.

When the data sub-set is a code noted used 0 or 1 times because of its value, the solution is the same:

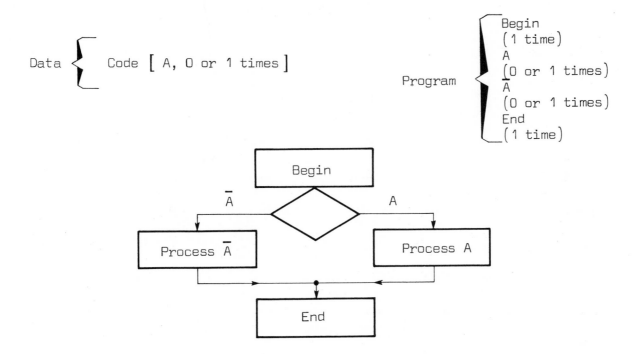

In this case it is frequent that both branches of the alternative involve processing and there is no null sequence.

DETAILED ORGANISATION

The rules for the detailed organisation given in the last chapter remain the same when the program includes sub-sets of alternative structure. However, it is important to note the position of branch instructions in an alternative structure:

- **An alternative structure has exactly one conditional branch instruction, which occurs at the end of the sequence 'begin' of the alternative,**
- **an alternative structure has as many unconditional branch instructions as terms to the alternative minus one. In an alternative structure with two terms the last instruction of one of them is an unconditional branch.**

A convention can be adopted whereby the sequences are numbered from top to bottom and from left to right on the flowchart. When the program is coded in the order of the sequence numbers, the unconditional branch terminates the sequences at the left as shown in the following flowchart.

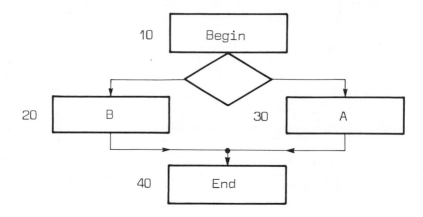

The unconditional branch terminates sequence 20 and ensures that the program continues into sequence 40.

ELEMENTARY PROGRAM STRUCTURES

Repetitive structures were studied in preceding chapters. In this chapter are given rules allowing alternative structures to be obtained. These two structures are the only ones which allow clear and optimal programs to be obtained.

Apart from the answer 1 time, there are only two answers to the question: how many times can a processing procedure be executed in a program set:

- N times making the execution repetitive,
- 0 or 1 times making the execution alternative.

All programs, however complex, can be built up by nesting, in hierarchical order, repetitive and alternative structures.

The problem where a process must be executed N times, N possibly 0, can be solved using cases already studied. Indeed, if a set of data is present A times in a set D and if A can be 0, the hierarchical organisation of the data is described as follows:

$$D \left\{ \begin{array}{l} \text{Group A} \\ \text{(0 or 1 times)} \end{array} \right. \left\{ \begin{array}{l} \text{Batch of data} \\ \text{(A times)} \end{array} \right.$$

The program is constructed by using the two rules already known:

- an alternative structure of the input data leads to an alternative structure of the program (used at the first level in this problem),
- a repetitive structure of the input data leads to a repetitive structure of the program (used at the second level in this problem).

Here is the diagram and flowchart:

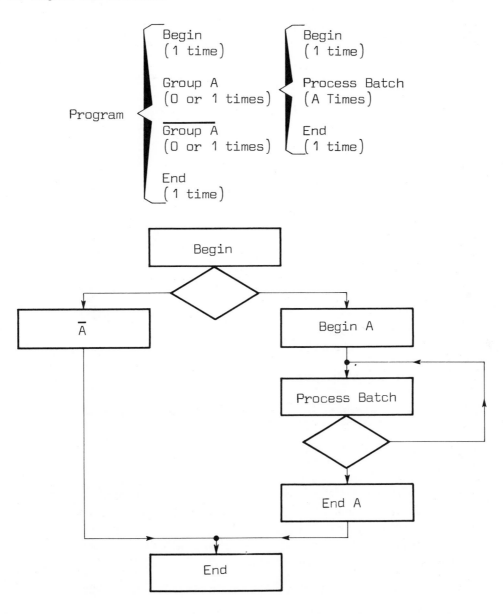

Here the term A of the alternative of the structure includes a repetitive structure.

RECAPITULATIVE EXAMPLE

The following example shows how to use the principal rules outlined up to now.

A periodic report of customers' accounts is to be produced. The input file contains for each customer a header record possibly followed by movements records. In other words there are 0, 1 or many movements for each customer. The layout of the output report is:

Customer N°	Name	MVT N°	DB MVT	
				CR MVT
Old Balance	New Balance		DB MVT Total	CR MVT Total
Customer N°	Name			
Old Balance	New Balance			
Customer N°	Name			

The layouts of the input records are:

Cust N°	Name	Old Balance

Cust N°	MVT N°	Amount	Code

The code can have 2 values and indicates whether the movement is a credit or a debit.
Suppose that, exceptionally, the input file could be empty: in this case no processing will take place and the next program in the suite will be initiated.
When there is processing, the debit total for each customer is calculated (DB) and also the credit total (CR), finally the new balance by the operations:

New balance = ± old balance — Sum of the debits + Sum of the Credits.

Assume that the signs of the old and new balance are obtained by using facilities offered by a high-level language. A customer who has no movements during the period in question must none the less be listed. Here is the diagram of the output:

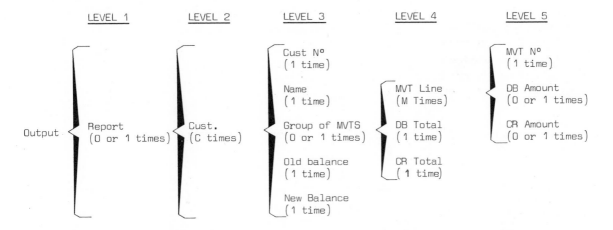

Note that the report is present 0 or 1 times since the input file can be empty. At level 3, the group of movements is noted (0 or 1 times), since a customer could have no movements whatsoever. The DB Total and CR Total are noted once per customer if he has any movements. When a total is zero spaces are output.

Here is the diagram of the hierarchical structure of the input data:

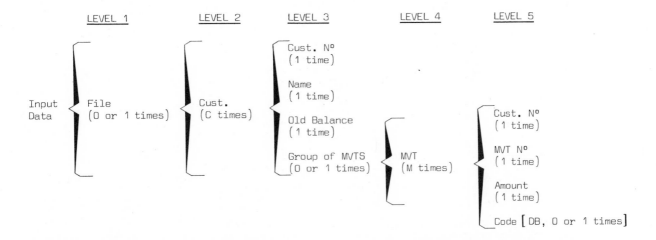

At Level 1, the file is noted 0 or 1 times since it could be empty. At Level 3, the group of movements could be present or absent. If it is present, it includes several movements. At Level 5, the code is

used 1 time but can take one of 2 values: DB, 0 or 1 times or $\overline{DB}$, 0 or 1 times. This code has to be tested according to the problem statement so code [DB, 0 or 1 times] is noted.
The program is constructed by applying the rules already known.

- Level 1 — alternative
- Level 2 — repetitive
- Level 3 — alternative
- Level 4 — repetitive
- Level 5 — alternative

The program diagram and flowchart of the logical sequences are as follows:

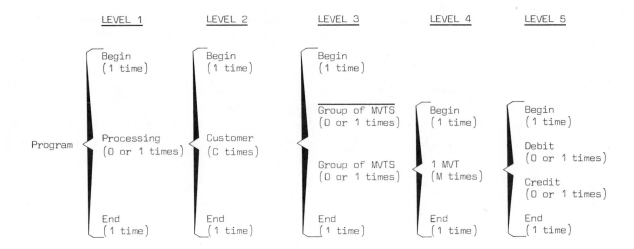

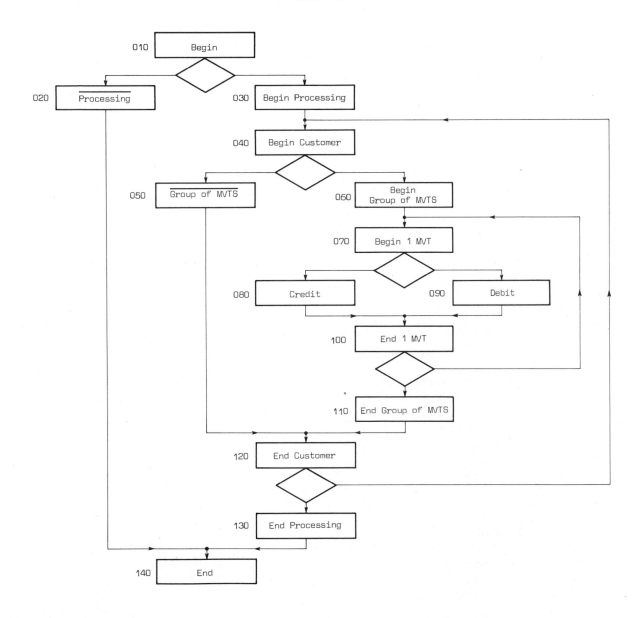

Here is the detailed organisation of the program. As regards the input instructions, a record should be read as many times as there are customers and movements plus 1 time for the end of file. *The practical means of locating input instructions is to ask the question : in which sequence has a record been processed?* A record must be read after the preceding one has been processed. In this example, a header record is processed once per customer in sequence 40 and a movement record in sequence 100. The first record of the file is read in sequence 10. Here is the list of the input instructions:

- 010 : read
- 040 : read
- 100 : read

List of branch instructions:

- 010 — if not end of file ($\overline{EOF}$)   030
- 020 —   140
- 040 — if Cust N° read = Cust N° processed   060
- 050 —   120
- 070 — if code DB   090
- 080 —   100
- 100 — if Cust N° read = Cust N° processed   070
- 120 — if not end of file ($\overline{EOF}$)   040

Note the unconditional branch instructions; there is one in each alternative structure: 020 to 140, 050 to 120, 080 to 100.

Preparation of branch instructions:

- 040 — transfer Cust N° to Reference Cust N° field

Calculations:

- 040 — Transfer old balance to working field
- 060 — Clear debit total field
- 060 — Clear credit total field
- 090 — Add debit to debit total
- 080 — Add credit to credit total
- 110 — Subtract debit total from working field
- 110 — Add credit total to working field

Outputs:

- 030 — Spaces to print area
- 040 — Transfer old balance to reference field
- 040 — Edit cust. heading
- 040 — Output and restore print area
- 070 — Edit MVT N°
- 090 — Edit debit amount
- 080 — Edit credit amount
- 100 — Output and restore print area
- 110 — Edit debit total
- 110 — Edit credit total
- 120 — Edit old balance from reference field
- 120 — Edit new balance from reference field
- 120 — Output and restore print area

In sequence 040, the old balance is transfered to a reference field. This item must be saved since it is read at the beginning of a customer but not used until the end of a customer.

The sorted list of instructions:

010 — Read
     If $\overline{EOF}$ 030
020 —   140
030 — Spaces to print area
040 — Cust N° to Reference Cust N°
     Old balance to working field
     „   „   ref field
     Edit Cust N°
     Print and restore print area
     Read
     If Cust N° = Ref. Cust N°   060
050 —   120
060 — Clear debit total
     Clear credit total
070 — Edit MVT N°
     If code DB   090

080 — Add credit to CR total
     Edit credit   100
090 — Add debit to DB total
     Edit debit
100 — Print and restore print area
     Read
     If cust N° = ref Cust N°   070
110 — Subtract DB total from
     working field
     Add CR total to working field
     Edit DB total
     Edit CR total
120 — Edit old balance
     Edit new balance
     Print and restore print area
     If $\overline{EOF}$ 040

In this program, sequences 020 and 050 contain no instructions: they are null sequences. The solution can be validated by using the output diagram.
The test data must allow each sequence to be executed even those that are null. A valid test package should allow each alternative to be executed as many times as there are terms but a different term each time and each repetitive to be executed at least twice.

SUMMARY

• *A results set of alternative structure includes one or more mutually exclusive sub-sets present 0 or 1 times.*

• *An input data set of alternative structure includes one or more mutually exclusive sub-sets utilized 0 or 1 times. The notation 0 or 1 can mean one of two things:*

   — *the sub-set is utilized 0 or 1 times*
   — *the sub-set is utilized 1 time but it is a code which must be tested and whose value is given: the value, noted in square brackets is utilized 0 or 1 times.*

• *A program set of alternative structure includes at least four sequences:*

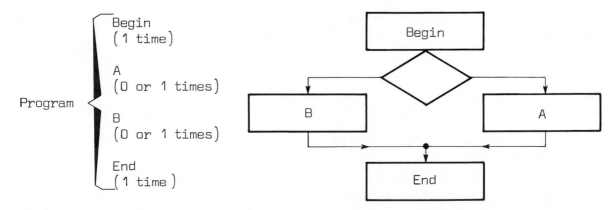

- *A program set of alternative structure always includes a conditional branch which terminates the sequence begin and as many unconditional branches as there are terms to the alternative minus one.*

- *A program set of alternative structure is obtained by applying the rule:*

— *If the input data structure is alternative, so is the corresponding program structure.*

EXERCISE

Quarterly statistics of ship movements for a maritime company.

RESULTS

REPORT

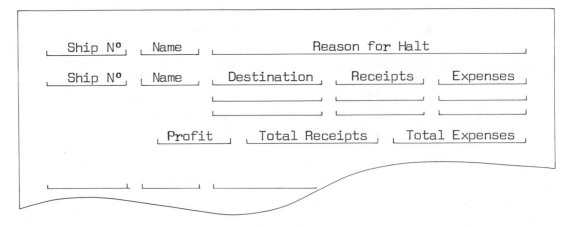

Only crossings completed by to-day's date are recorded.

DATA

Card file sorted by ship N°; for each ship there is a header card followed by either a halt card or a group of crossing cards.

Header card: 1 per ship (error conditions excluded)

Halt card: 0 or 1 per Ship:

Crossing card: 0 or many per Ship:

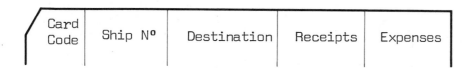

Processing: calculate total Receipts and Expenses and Profit = Total Receipts — Total Expenses. (A Loss is recorded as a negative Profit.)

Do the complete organisation of this problem (results, data, program and detailed organisation).

SOLUTION

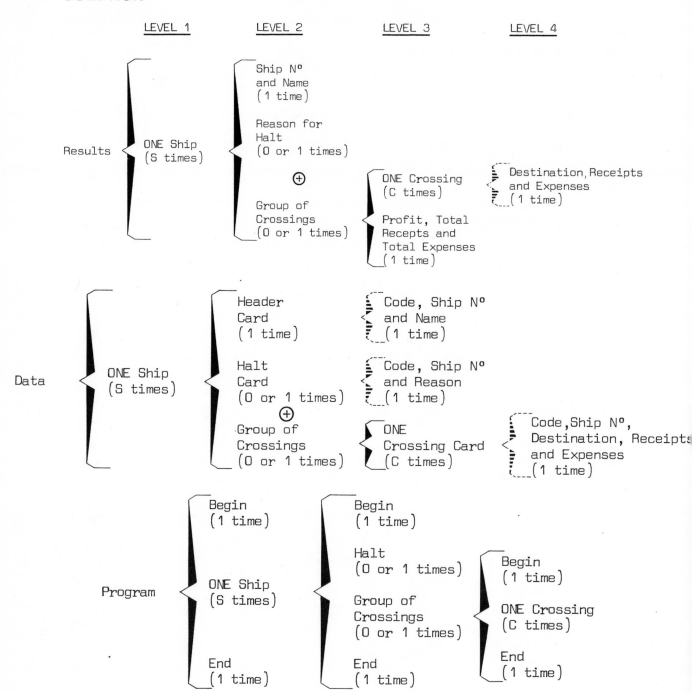

LEVEL 1   LEVEL 2   LEVEL 3   LEVEL 4

Results — ONE Ship (S times) —
- Ship N° and Name (1 time)
- Reason for Halt (0 or 1 times) ⊕
- Group of Crossings (0 or 1 times) —
  - ONE Crossing (C times) — Destination, Receipts and Expenses (1 time)
  - Profit, Total Receipts and Total Expenses (1 time)

Data — ONE Ship (S times) —
- Header Card (1 time) — Code, Ship N° and Name (1 time)
- Halt Card (0 or 1 times) — Code, Ship N° and Reason (1 time) ⊕
- Group of Crossings (0 or 1 times) — ONE Crossing Card (C times) — Code, Ship N°, Destination, Receipts and Expenses (1 time)

Program — ONE Ship (S times) —
- Begin (1 time)
- ONE Ship (S times) —
  - Begin (1 time)
  - Halt (0 or 1 times)
  - Group of Crossings (0 or 1 times) —
    - Begin (1 time)
    - ONE Crossing (C times)
    - End (1 time)
  - End (1 time)
- End (1 time)

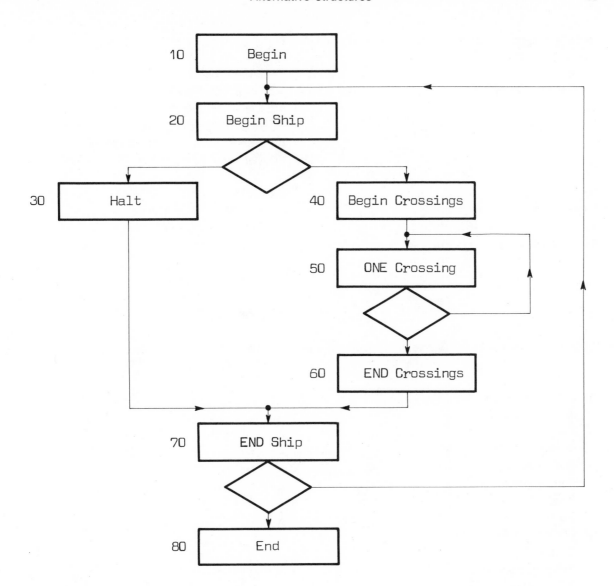

Detailed organisation: Instruction Lists by Type

Read

10 Read 1st Card
20 Read
30 Read
50 Read

Branch

20 If crossing card	40
30	70
50 If crossing card	50
70 If EOF	20

Calculations

40 Clear Tot. Receipts
40 Clear Tot. Expenses
50 Add Receipts to Tot. Receipts
50 Add Expenses to Tot. Expenses
60 Calculate Profit = Tot. Rec. — Tot. Exp.

Outputs

20 Edit Ship N° and Name
20 Print and Restore
30 Edit Reason
50 Edit Destination, Receipts and Expenses
50 Print and Restore
60 Edit Tot. Receipts and Total Expenses
60 Print and Restore

Detailed organisation: Sorted Instruction List in Sequences

10 Read 1st card
20 Edit Ship N° and Name
 Print and Restore
 Read
 If crossing card   40
30 Edit Reason
 Print and Restore
 Read
 Go to   70
40 Clear Total Receipts
 Clear Total Expenses
50 Add Receipts to Tot. Rec.
 Add Expenses to Tot. Exp.
 Edit Destination, Receipts and Expenses
 Print and Restore
 Read
 If crossing card   50
60 Calculate Profit
 Edit Total line
 Print and Restore
70 If EOF   20
80 Stop

6 — COMPLEX STRUCTURES

In the preceding chapters the elementary structures for data, programs and results were dealt with:

- repetitive structure,
- alternative structure.

It is now possible to discuss sets of complex structure:

- complex repetitive structure,
- complex alternative structure,
- complex mixed structure.

A data set of complex structure includes several elementary alternative or repetitive structures at the first level of subdivision of the set considered as universal.

Likewise, a program set of complex structure is an ordered string of elementary structures. Each elementary structure includes a sub-set 'begin' and a sub-set 'end'. In a complex structure, the sub-set 'end' of the first elementary structure is immediately followed by a sub-set 'begin' of the next elementary structure. These two sub-sets, 'end' of the structure that precedes and 'begin' of the structure the follows, are executed 1 time within the set, at the same place in the program and thus merge to constitute a single logical sequence which is named 'intermediate' (abbreviation 'Int.').

An 'intermediate' sequence in a complex program set replaces the 'end' of the elementary structure that precedes and the 'begin' of that which follows.

A complex structure includes two or more elementary structures. The number of intermediate sequences in a complex program set is equal to the number of elementary structures at the highest level of this set minus one.

The repetitive and mixed complex structures will be dealt with in this chapter. The complex alternative structure, which poses special problems, will be developed in PART II of this book.

COMPLEX REPETITIVE STRUCTURES

A data set of complex repetitive structure includes several elementary repetitive structures at the first level of subdivision of the set considered as universal.

Recall that the repetition concerns the *utilization* or *presence* of information when dealing with input or output sets respectively. It concerns the *execution* of a series of procedures programmed one time when dealing with a program set.

OUTPUT DATA

A results set of complex repetitive structures includes several types of sub-set present several times at the first level of subdivision of the set.

Example: An annual report, by customer, of orders received and invoices sent by an enterprise:

```
┌─────────────────────────────────────────────────────────────────────────┐

    Cust. N°              Order N°               Amount of Order
  └───────────┘         └───────────┘         └───────────────────────┘

                        └───────────┘         └───────────────────────┘

                        └───────────┘         └───────────────────────┘
                                                Total Amounts of  Orders
                        Invoice N°              Amount of Invoice
                      └───────────┘         └───────────────────────┘

                        └───────────┘         └───────────────────────┘
                                                Total Amounts of Invoices


  └───────────┘         └───────────┘         └───────────────────────┘
```

Here is the diagram for the results:

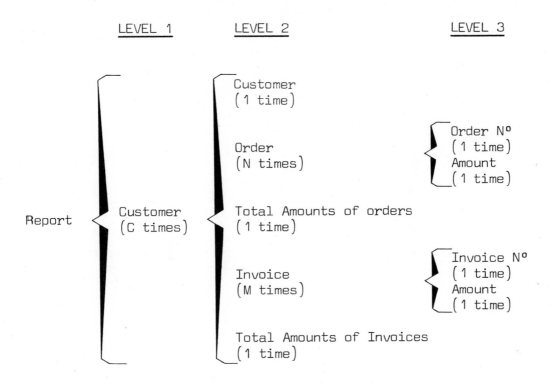

LEVEL 1   LEVEL 2   LEVEL 3

Report { Customer (C times) {
    Customer (1 time)
    Order (N times) { Order N° (1 time) / Amount (1 time) }
    Total Amounts of orders (1 time)
    Invoice (M times) { Invoice N° (1 time) / Amount (1 time) }
    Total Amounts of Invoices (1 time)
}

At the customer level, the results structure is complex repetitive.

INPUT DATA

An input data set of complex structure includes several types of sub-set, each utilized several times at the first level of subdivision of the set considered as universal.

Examples: Take the input file required for the report presented above: this file, sorted in ascending order on the customer N°, contains, for each customer:

- several order records (at least 1)
- several invoice records (at least 1)

Code	Customer N°	Order N°	Amount

Code	Customer N°	Invoice N°	Amount

Here is the diagram for the input data:

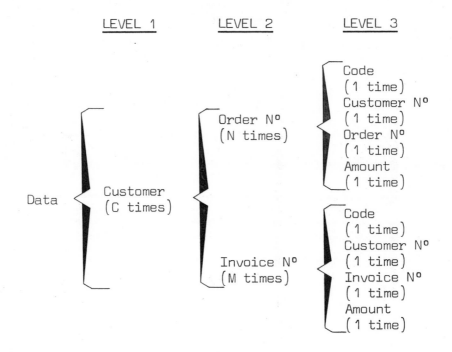

At level 2, customer level, the data structure is complex repetitive.

THE PROGRAM

A program set of complex repetitive structure includes several sub-sets executed in a repetitive manner at the first level of subdivision of the set considered as universal.

A program complex repetitive structure corresponds to an input data complex repetitive structure by repeated application of the rule: when the input data structure is repetitive so is the corresponding program structure.

The number of repetitive sub-sets of the program is equal to the number of repetitive structures of data.

A program set of complex repetitive structure includes as many intermediate sequences as there are elementary structures at this level minus one.

Example: Here is the input data diagram again:

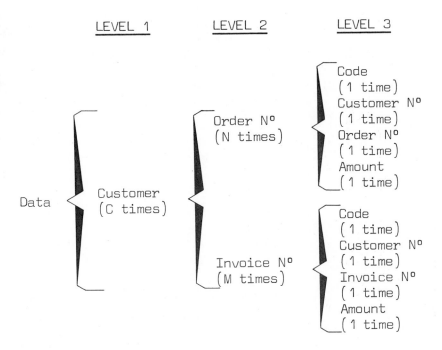

Here is the program diagram:

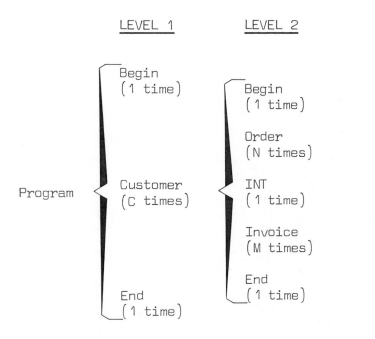

Here is the sequence flowchart of the program:

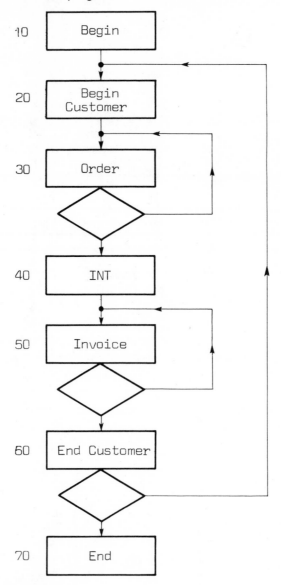

DETAILED ORGANISATION

Only the operations to be executed in the sequence 'intermediate' (40) will be detailed here. This sequence replaces 2 sub-sets:

- the sub-set 'end' of the repetitive structure 'ORDERS',
- the sub-set 'begin' of the repetitive structure 'INVOICES'.

The sub-set 'end ORDERS' contains the instructions to output the total amount of orders.

- edit total amounts of orders,
- print and restore print area.

The sub-set 'begin INVOICES' contains an instruction to initialise the invoices total:

- Clear total invoices field.

Here is the complete organisation of the sequence 40:

- 40 INT. Edit total amounts of orders
  Print and restore print area
  Clear total invoices field.

COMPLEX MIXED STRUCTURES

A data set of complex mixed structure includes several elementary structures, some repetitive and the others alternative.

RESULTS

An output results set of complex mixed structure includes several types of sub-set some alternative and the others repetitive, at the first level of subdivision of the set considered as universal.

Example: take a periodical statistical report of amounts of invoices sent to customers of an enterprise. This report contains one line for each amount followed by a total line. Certain customers have had a discount and others not. The discount depends on the customer.

Report layout:

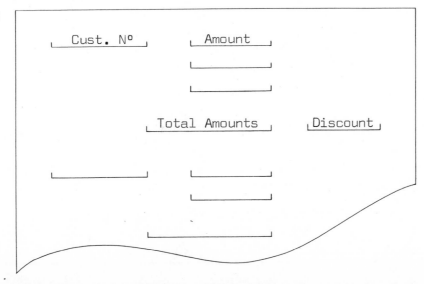

Here is the results diagram:

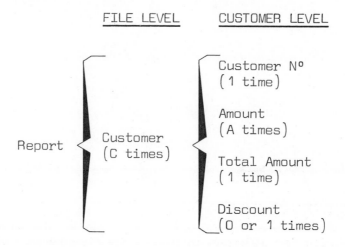

At the customer level, the data structure is complex mixed since for each customer, the amounts are output repetitively and the discount is an alternative output: discount or nothing at all.

INPUT DATA

An input data set of complex mixed structure includes several types of sub-set, some alternative and the others repetitive, at the first level of subdivision of the set considered as universal.

Example: Take the input file which could be used to obtain the report outlined above. This file, sorted by customer N° includes for each customer several invoice records, at least one, possibly followed by a discount record.

Customer N°	Amount	Code

Customer N°	% Discount	Code

Here is the diagram of the input data:

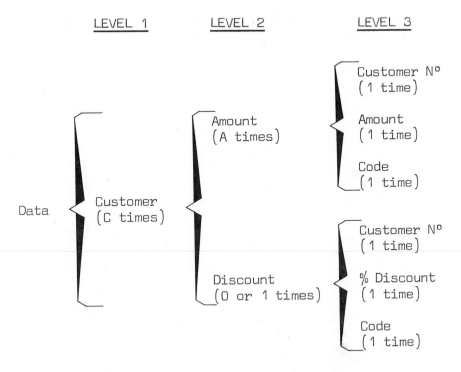

At the second level, the data set is complex mixed since the utilization of the amounts is repetitive and that of the discount is random (alternative).

THE PROGRAM

A program set of complex mixed structure includes several sub-sets, some executed in a repetitive manner, the others in an alternative manner at the first level of subdivision of the set considered as universal.

A program complex mixed structure corresponds to a complex mixed input data structure, by repeated application of the rules: the program structure is repetitive (alternative) when the data structure is repetitive (alternative).

However, when several alternatives follow each other, the rules outlined in Part II of this book must be applied (complex alternative structure). The number of elementary program structures is equal to the number of elementary input data structures except in the case where certain rules for complex alternative structures have been applied. A program complex mixed structure includes as many intermediate sequences as there are elementary structures minus one.

Example: Here is the input data diagram again:

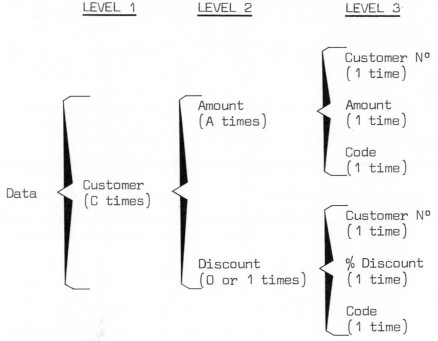

Here is the program diagram:

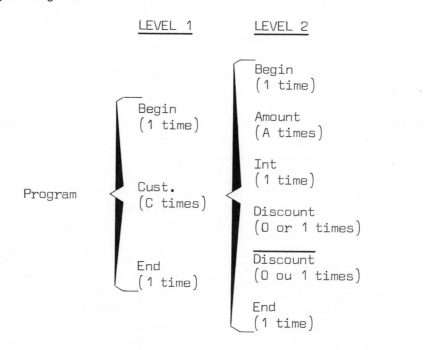

Flowchart of the logical sequences:

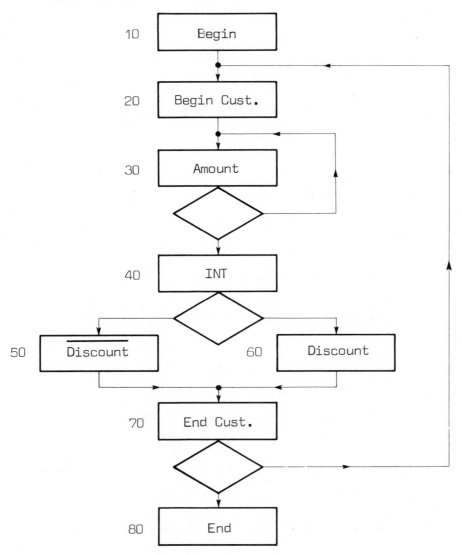

DETAILED ORGANISATION OF THE SEQUENCES BEGIN AND END

The sequences 'begin' and 'end' in complex mixed structures have two functions:

- Begin (or End) of the set,
- Begin (or End) of the first (or last) elementary structure.

The different functions of the same sequence can be separated in order to facilitate later amendments.

Example: Take the customer set just treated. The sequence 20: begin customer, has the function of beginning the customer set. Hence the instruction:

- 20 Edit Customer N°.

This same sequence also has the function of beginning the repetitive structure of the processing of the amounts. Hence the instruction:

- 20 clear total amounts field.

Sequence 20 is finally programmed in the order:

- 20 begin customer • Edit Customer N°
                      • Clear Total Amounts field.

SUMMARY

- *A data set of complex structure includes several elementary structures, alternatives or repetitives at the first level of subdivision of the set considered as universal.*

- *When the complex structure includes only elementary repetitive (alternative, both) structures, it is called a complex repetitive (alternative, mixed) structure.*

- *The rules for constructing the program from the input data structure can be applied to complex structures except in the case of several succeeding alternatives.*

- *A complex program structure always includes:*
  - *a begin sub-set which functions simultaneously as the beginning for the set and for the first elementary structure,*
  - *as many intermediate sequences as there are elementary structures minus one. An intermediate sequence functions as the end of the previous elementary structure and as the beginning of that following,*
  - *an end subset which functions as the ending of the last elementary structure and also as that of the set as a whole.*

EXERCISE

Statements of orders accepted.

RESULTS

REPORT

Customer N°	Name Address		
Product N°	Quantity	Unit Price	Value
	Discount	Total Value (Gross)	
		Total Value (Net)	

When a customer has no discount, the Total Value (Net) is set equal to the Total Value (Gross).

DATA

The input is sequentially organised so that each customer record is immediately followed by P product records (error conditions excluded):

Customer N°	Name Address	Discount %

Product N°	Quantity	Unit Price	Value

PROCESSING

- Accumulate the values giving Total Value (Gross) for each customer
- If the Discount % > 0, calculate the Discount and Total Value (Net) = Total Value (Gross) — Discount
- If the Discount % Not > 0, then set Total Value (Net) = Total Value (Gross).

Organise this program into logical sequences and then do the detailed organisation.

SOLUTION

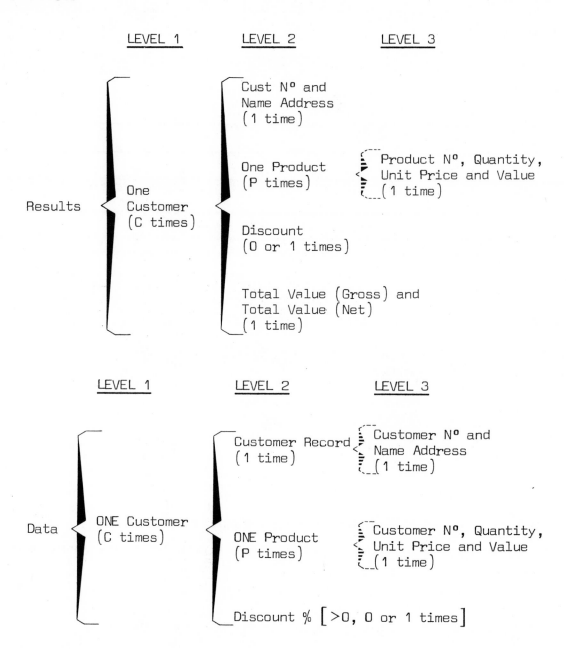

Note that the discount % is placed after the product records because this data item is used after the processing of the product records.

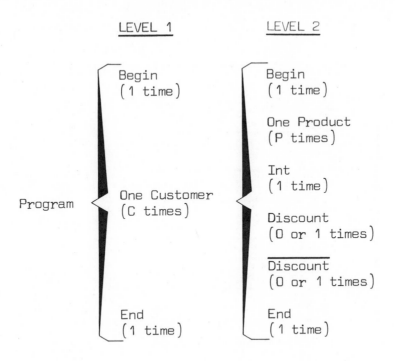

LEVEL 1

Program
- Begin (1 time)
- One Customer (C times)
- End (1 time)

LEVEL 2

- Begin (1 time)
- One Product (P times)
- Int (1 time)
- Discount (0 or 1 times)
- Discount (0 or 1 times)
- End (1 time)

Flowchart:

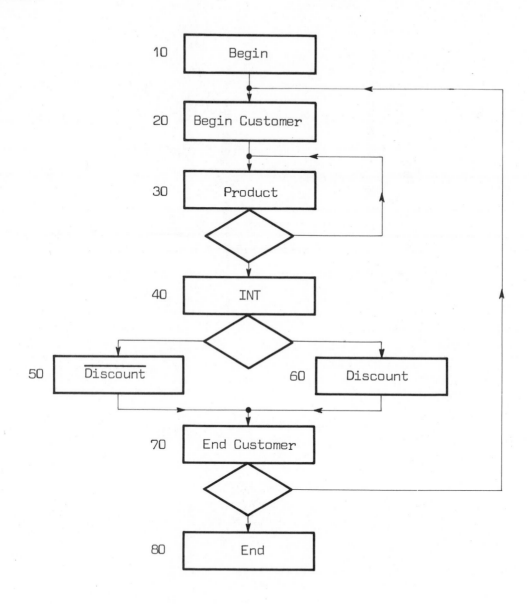

Detailed organisation: Instruction Lists by Type

Read
10 Read 1st Record
20 Read
30 Read

Branch

30	If Cust. N° = Ref	30
40	If Disct Rate > 0	60
50	Go to	70
70	If $\overline{EOF}$	20

Preparation of Branch
20 Transfer Cust. N° to Ref

Calculations + Preparation of
20 Transfer Disct. % to Disct. Rate
20 Clear Total Value (Gross)
30 Add Value to Total Value (Gross)
60 Calculate Discount = Tot. Val. (Gross) × Disct. Rate
60 Calculate Tot. Value (Net) = Tot. Val (Gross) — Discount

Output
20 Edit Cust N°, Name Address
20 Print and Restore
30 Edit Product Line
30 Print and Restore
40 Edit Tot. Value (Gross)
50 Print and Restore
50 Edit Tot. Value (Net) = Tot. Value (Gross)
60 Edit Discount
60 Print and Restore
60 Edit Tot. Value (Net)
70 Print and Restore

Detailed organisation: Sorted Instruction List in Sequences

10	Read 1st record	
20	Transfer Cust. N° to Ref.	
	Transfer Disct. % to Disct. Rate	
	Clear Total Value (Gross)	
	Edit Cust N°, Name Address	
	Print and Restore	
	Read	
30	Add Value to total Value (Gross)	
	Edit Product line	
	Print and Restore	
	Read	
	If Cust. N° = Ref	30
40	Edit Tot. Value (Gross)	
	If Disct. Rate > 0	60

50	Print and Restore	
	Edit Tot. Value (Net) = Total Value (Gross)	
	Go to	70
60	Calculate Discount	
	Edit Discount	
	Print and Restore	
	Calculate Total Value (Net) = Total Value (Gross) — Discount	
	Edit Tot. Value (Net)	
70	Print and Restore	
	If EOF	20
80	Stop	

CONCLUSION OF PART 1

The informatician is above all concerned with the organisation of data sets. He has to outline the hierarchical logical structure of the data in the results and the data which are input to the program set studied. He constructs the program which is also a data file. The program is constructed from the inputs and is validated from the outputs. In preparing the data to obtain the results he can give priority neither to the inputs, nor to the outputs nor to the procedures. He has to keep all three in mind.

The preceding chapters have shown to begin with that in order one must:

- define the hierarchical structure of the results,
- define the hierarchical structure of the input while bearing in mind the results and the processing directives,
- organise the program from the inputs and validate it from the outputs.

The program is organised in two stages:

— construction of the program in hierarchical sub-sets which leads to a definition of the program as an ordered set of logical sequences,
— detailed organisation.

At every stage, the reasoning involved is hierarchical, and starts from the set at the highest level. The final stage is a space-time representation of the solution: the flowchart of the logical sequences. The hierarchical organisation makes it clear that there are only two elementary structures:

— repetitive structure,
— alternative structure.

Any organisation in which other structures are used is unclear and nearly always has bad performance. Bringing the organisation of the program back to the two elementary structures always yields a more economical organisation and always speeds up debugging and maintenance.

PART II

THE OPTIMISATION OF PROGRAMS AND THE PROCESSING PHASES

1 — INPUT DATA OF COMPLEX ALTERNATIVE STRUCTURE AND TREE STRUCTURES

A data set of complex alternative structure includes several sub-sets present or utilised 0 or 1 times and which are not mutually exclusive.

To indicate that sub-sets are not mutually exclusive, the symbol + (set union) will be used on the diagrams.

Example: The input data set concerning the raw material stock of an enterprise.

Physical files:
Old Stock — 0 or 1 records per product.

Product N⁰	Information

Movement — 0 or 1 records per product.

Product N⁰	Information

Diagram for the input data:

$$
\text{Data} \left\{ \begin{array}{c} \text{Product} \\ (\text{P times}) \end{array} \right. \left\{ \begin{array}{c} \text{Old Stock} \\ (\text{0 or 1 times}) \\ + \\ \text{Movement} \\ (\text{0 or 1 times}) \end{array} \right.
$$

PROCESSING USING TREE STRUCTURES

The first two elementary rules for constructing programs from the hierarchical structure of the input data are now familiar:

1. **If the input data structure is repetitive, so is the corresponding program structure.**

2. **If the input data structure is alternative, so is the corresponding program structure.**

Here is the third and last elementary rule:

3. **When the input data includes a complex alternative structure, a truth table must be drawn up with whose aid the program will be constructed.**

These three rules can be summed up as follows:

The structure of a program is identical to the structure of the input data except in the case where the input data have a complex alternative structure. In this case a truth table should be drawn up.

When writing out the truth table, the relevant universal set should be noted at the top left of the table. The corresponding universal set in the results set must then be identified. The procedures required to obtain the results present 0 or 1 times within this set are actions to be noted in the table.

Example: Take the following diagrams for input and results concerning the stock program.

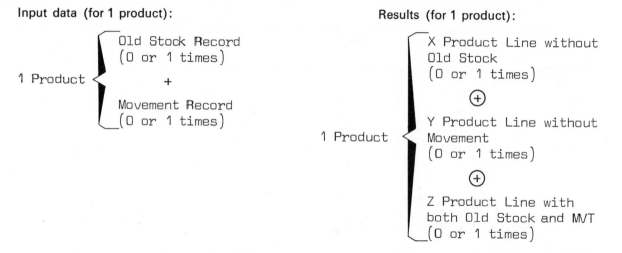

Input data (for 1 product):

1 Product
  - Old Stock Record (0 or 1 times)
  - +
  - Movement Record (0 or 1 times)

Results (for 1 product):

1 Product
  - X Product Line without Old Stock (0 or 1 times)
  - ⊕
  - Y Product Line without Movement (0 or 1 times)
  - ⊕
  - Z Product Line with both Old Stock and M/T (0 or 1 times)

The 'product' set is a data set of complex alternative structure. Thus a truth table is drawn up. In the truth table the set $\overline{O}.\overline{M}$ is null. Action X is performed on the data set $\overline{O}.M$, action Y on the set $O.\overline{M}$, and action Z on the set O.M.

1 Product O M	X	Y	Z
0 0	φ	φ	φ
0 1	X		
1 0		X	
1 1			X

ACTIONS PERFORMED ON DISJOINT OR WHOLLY INCLUDED DATA SETS

RULE 1

When the data sub-sets subject to the actions noted in the truth table are disjoint or wholly included, the optimal program structure is a tree structure.

RULE 2

When a results sub-set can be obtained by several different actions, the results diagram should be completed by listing in square brackets, next to the results sub-set, the different actions from which it can be obtained.

RULE 3

When several actions give rise to the same output procedure (i.e. when the Boolean expression for the output procedure is the union of a number of minterms), it must be considered initially that there are as many output procedures as actions. Afterwards the output procedures common to several actions can be regrouped when simplification allows this.

RULE 4

The set $\overline{R}$, ($\overline{\text{Results}}$) of information for which there is no output should always be described. Indeed, when $\overline{R}$ is not null, 'not to output results' is an action which should appear in the columns of the truth table in the same way as the actions for the output and preparation of results.

Example: A bonus is to be calculated for different categories of the personnel of an enterprise. The input data is a file with one record for each employee.

		Codes	
Employee N°	Name	A	B

Code A is for employees with one or more years of past service. Code $\overline{A}$ corresponds to those with less than one year's service. Code B is management staff ($\overline{B}$ for the others).[*] Management employees having less than one year's service do not receive a bonus. The other management employees receive a bonus P_1. The ordinary employees with less than one year's service receive a bonus P_2 and the others a bonus P_3.
The result required is a list of the employees receiving a bonus, one employee per line.

[*] Note for readers in countries other than France, the management employees in France are subject to special rules as regards remuneration.

Results diagram:

Here rules 2 and 4 have been applied. The set of the N_1 employees receiving a bonus is the complement of the set of the N_2 employees not receiving a bonus. The universal set is the set of all (N) the employees of the enterprise where:

$$N = N_1 + N_2$$

In the set of the N_1 employees receiving a bonus the origins of the amount of bonus have been listed in square brackets: $[P_1, P_2, P_3]$.

Input diagram:

The first level of the program is obtained by applying the rules for repetitive structures.

At the second level, a truth table is drawn up. The actions are obtained from the results diagram (R) and the results diagram (R̄).

1 Employee A B	Print Bonus	P1	P2	P3	No Output
0 0	X		X		
0 1					X
1 0	X			X	
1 1	X	X			

The data sub-sets subject to the different actions are disjoint and/or wholly included:

- Print bonus and No output are disjoint
- P_1, P_2 and P_3 are disjoint
- P_1, P_2 and P_3 are all wholly included in Edit Bonus.

The program should thus be constructed using a tree structure.

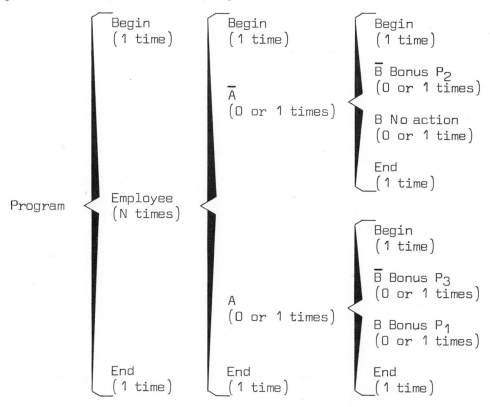

The flowchart is as follows:

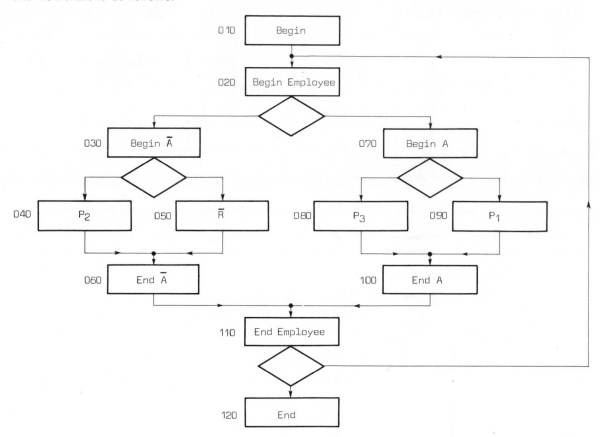

Every times a bonus is calculated, a line must be printed. Whatever the amounts are, the output operations are the same and must be programmed several times or else a sub-routine must be written to be called in these sequences if this should prove more economical. In any case to find an optimal solution, the Boolean expression for the printing must be examined. Printing occurs for the sub-set of employees:

'Print bonus' (say) $= \overline{A}.\overline{B} + A.\overline{B} + A.B$

Since the test A is the first in the tree structure, the simplification is done as follows:

$$\begin{aligned} \text{Print Bonus} &= \overline{A}.\overline{B} + A.\overline{B} + A.B \\ &= \overline{A}.\overline{B} + A.(\overline{B} + B) \\ &= \overline{A}.\overline{B} + A.(1) \\ &= \overline{A}.\overline{B} + A \end{aligned}$$

(Note: by convention the data set subject to a given action X will be called the set X e.g. above, the data set subject to the action 'Print bonus' is also called 'Print bonus'.)

The printing or the calling of the sub-routine must be programmed in the sequence executed for the set $\overline{A}.\overline{B}$ (sequence 040) and in the sequence executed for the set A but at the end (sequence 100). Everything occurs as if there were two print instructions (cf. Rule 3):

Print 1 = $\overline{A}.\overline{B}$
Print 2 = A

RULE

When, after simplification, the Boolean expression for a set subject to an action is the union of N sets, this action must be considered as N identical independent actions.

In practice, the application of this rule amounts to the replacing of the N identical actions by N sub-routine calls.

SIMPLIFICATION OF TREE STRUCTURES

To each action in the truth table corresponds a data sub-set upon which it is to be performed. These data sub-sets, expressed as an union of minterms, must be simplified by using Boolean algebra or otherwise. In practice, the simplification should be done in at least two different ways to avoid mistakes (for example by Boolean algebra and by a Karnaugh map). Indeed, time and energy must be spent on verifications during the construction of a program. This investment yields a hundredfold during the debugging period. Once the Boolean expressions have been simplified, the tree structure can be optimised.

To do this, the Boolean expressions of the data sub-sets subject to the actions are listed. By using the commutative property of Boolean algebra, the simple sub-sets (single letters) are ordered in each expression from left to right according to the frequency of appearance with the most frequently used at the left. Thus will the skeleton of the tree structure emerge.

Example: Take a table for the sub-sets A,B,C,D of a set DATA of data and the actions V,W,X,Y,Z and $\overline{R}$:

DATA A B C D	V	W	X	Y	Z	$\overline{R}$
0 0 0 0						X
0 0 0 1						X
0 0 1 0	X			X		
0 0 1 1	X			X		
0 1 0 0						X
0 1 0 1						X
0 1 1 0	X				X	
0 1 1 1	X				X	
1 0 0 0						X
1 0 0 1						X
1 0 1 0	X	X	X			
1 0 1 1	X	X	X			
1 1 0 0						X
1 1 0 1						X
1 1 1 0	X	X				
1 1 1 1	X	X				

Simplification of the expressions and verifications:

$V = \overline{A}.\overline{B}.C.\overline{D} + \overline{A}.\overline{B}.C.D + \overline{A}.B.C.\overline{D} + \overline{A}.B.C.D + A.\overline{B}.C.\overline{D} + A.\overline{B}.C.D + A.B.C.\overline{D} + A.B.C.D$

$= \overline{A}.\overline{B}.C\ (\overline{D} + D) + \overline{A}.B.C\ (\overline{D} + D) + A.\overline{B}.C\ (\overline{D} + D) + A.B.C + (\overline{D} + D)$

$= \overline{A}.\overline{B}.C\ (1) + \overline{A}.B.C\ (1) + A.\overline{B}.C\ (1) + A.B.C\ (1)$

$= \overline{A}.\overline{B}.C + \overline{A}.B.C + A.\overline{B}.C + A.B.C$

$= \overline{A}.C\ (\overline{B} + B) + A.C\ (\overline{B} + B)$

$= \overline{A}.C\ (1) + A.C\ (1)$

$= \overline{A}.C + A.C$

$= C\ (\overline{A} + A)$

$= C\ (1)$

$= C$

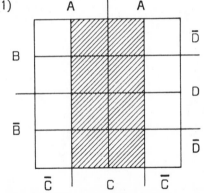

$W = A.\bar{B}.C.\bar{D} + A.\bar{B}.C.D + A.B.C.\bar{D} + A.B.C.D$
$= A.\bar{B}.C \,(\bar{D} + D) + A.B.C \,(\bar{D} + D)$
$= A.\bar{B}.C \,(1) + A.B.C \,(1)$
$= A.\bar{B}.C + A.B.C$
$= A.C \,(\bar{B} + B)$
$= A.C \,(1)$
$= A.C$

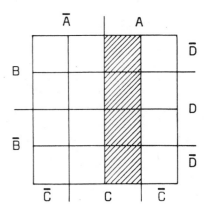

$X = A.\bar{B}.C.\bar{D} + A.\bar{B}.C.D$
$= A.\bar{B}.C \,(\bar{D} + D)$
$= A.\bar{B}.C \,(1)$
$= A.\bar{B}.C$

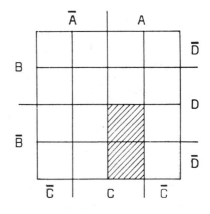

$Y = \bar{A}.\bar{B}.C.\bar{D} + \bar{A}.\bar{B}.C.D$
$= \bar{A}.\bar{B}.C \,(\bar{D} + D)$
$= \bar{A}.\bar{B}.C \,(1)$
$= \bar{A}.\bar{B}.C$

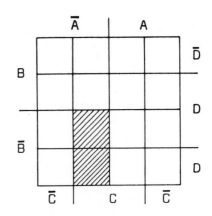

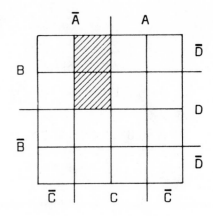

$$Z = \overline{A}.B.C.\overline{D} + \overline{A}.B.C.D$$
$$= \overline{A}.B.C\ (\overline{D} + D)$$
$$= \overline{A}.B.C\ (1)$$
$$= \overline{A}.B.C$$

$$\overline{R} = \overline{A}.\overline{B}.\overline{C}.\overline{D} + \overline{A}.\overline{B}.\overline{C}.D + \overline{A}.B.\overline{C}.\overline{D} + \overline{A}.B.\overline{C}.D + A.\overline{B}.\overline{C}.\overline{D} + A.\overline{B}.\overline{C}.D +$$
$$A.B.\overline{C}.D + A.B.\overline{C}.\overline{D}$$
$$= \overline{A}.\overline{B}.\overline{C}\ (\overline{D} + D) + \overline{A}.B.\overline{C}\ (\overline{D} + D) + A.\overline{B}.\overline{C}\ (\overline{D} + D) + A.B.\overline{C}\ (\overline{D} + D)$$
$$= \overline{A}.\overline{B}.\overline{C}\ (1) + \overline{A}.B.\overline{C}\ (1) + A.\overline{B}.\overline{C}\ (1) + A.B.\overline{C}\ (1)$$
$$= \overline{A}.\overline{B}.\overline{C} + \overline{A}.B.\overline{C} + A.\overline{B}.\overline{C} + A.B.\overline{C}$$
$$= \overline{A}.\overline{C}\ (\overline{B} + B) + A.\overline{C}\ (\overline{B} + B)$$
$$= \overline{A}.\overline{C}\ (1) + A.\overline{C}\ (1)$$
$$= \overline{A}.\overline{C} + A.\overline{C}$$
$$= \overline{C}\ (\overline{A} + A)$$
$$= \overline{C}\ (1)$$
$$= \overline{C}$$

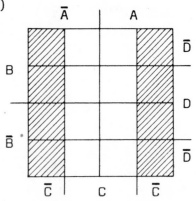

Ordered list of the simplified expressions:

$$V = C$$
$$W = C.A$$
$$X = C.A.\bar{B}$$
$$Y = C.\bar{A}.\bar{B}$$
$$Z = C.\bar{A}.B$$
$$\bar{R} = \bar{C}$$

Diagram of the corresponding program sub-set P constructed using a tree structure to process the sub-set DATA of data:

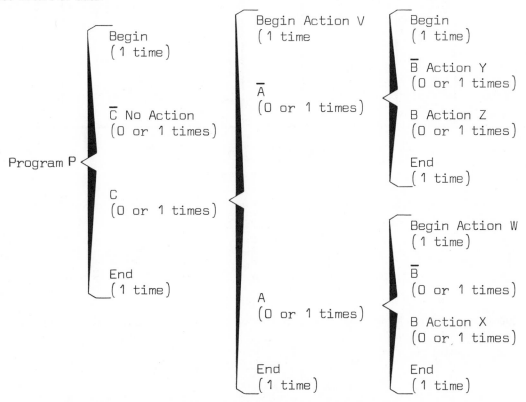

In the solution obtained, there are 4 conditional branch instructions (tests). Recall that the number of tests in a non-simplified tree structure is equal to the number of minterms minus 1, i.e. 15 in this example.

To avoid errors while using a Karnaugh map, it is advisable to note the decimal (or octal or hexadecimal) equivalent of the binary number corresponding to each minterm at the left of the truth table. This number can also be marked in the corresponding square of the map.

It is a good idea to have preprinted truth tables and maps for up to 6 sets.

Example: Table and Map for 3 data sets A, B, C and one action X.

	E A B C	X				
0	0 0 0	X				
1	0 0 1	X				
2	0 1 0					
3	0 1 1					
4	1 0 0	X				
5	1 0 1					
6	1 1 0	X				
7	1 1 1	X				

Karnaugh map before use:

The squares to be marked for action X are Nᵒˢ 0, 1, 4, 6 and 7. The diagram after marking action X is:

Simplified expression for the data sub-set subject to action X:

$$X = \overline{A}.\overline{B} + A.\,(B + \overline{B}.\overline{C})$$

CODES THAT CAN TAKE N VALUES

The codes used up to now have been binary codes which allow a set and its complement to be identified. Now codes, identifiers etc.... that can determine more than 2 sets must be studied.

RULE

To distinguish N sets, the number of binary codes required is equal to the exponent of the power of 2 equal to or greater than N.

RULE

The number of disjoint sets corresponding to N binary codes is equal to 2^N.

By applying these rules, codes taking more than 2 values can be converted into binary codes which allow a truth table to be compiled.

Example: The quantity of each product in a stock of raw materials is used as a code in a program for restocking:

- if the quantity is < 0, an error condition is indicated,
- if the quantity is non-negative and < minimum stock an order for restocking must be sent out,
- if the quantity is greater than or equal to minimum stock, no output is produced.

The value of the stock quantity allow 3 categories to be distinguished. The power of 2 greater than or equal to 3 is $4 = 2^2$. Thus, the quantity is converted into 2 binary codes:

— N : quantity < 0
— M : quantity < minimum stock

Truth table for one product P:

P		ERR	RESTOCK	$\overline{R}$
N	M			
0	0			X
0	1		X	
1	0	φ	φ	φ
1	1	X		

The sub-set $N.\overline{M}$ is null: The quantity cannot be both negative and greater than minimum stock. The program is constructed with a tree structure by applying the rules already set out. The null set can be used in the simplification.

$$\overline{R} = \overline{N}.\overline{M} + N.\overline{M}$$
$$= \overline{M}. (\overline{N} + N)$$
$$= \overline{M}. (1)$$
$$= \overline{M}$$

List of data sub-sets subject to the actions:

$$\overline{R} \qquad\quad = \overline{M}$$
$$RESTOCK = M.\overline{N}$$
$$ERR \qquad = M.N$$

Diagram of the program structure:

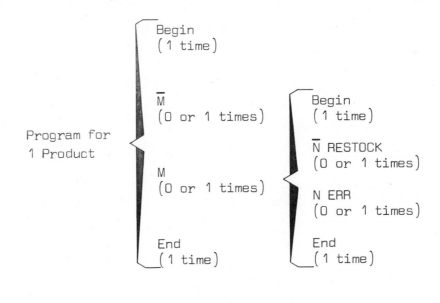

Flowchart of the logical sequences:

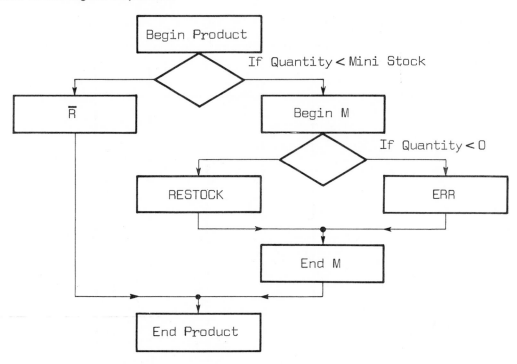

On the flowchart the tests have been marked.

SUMMARY

- *When the input data set includes a complex alternative structure, a truth table must be drawn up with whose aid the program will be constructed.*

- *When the data sub-sets subject to the different actions are disjoint or wholly included the optimal structure is a tree structure.*

- *Actions noted on the results and results diagrams should also appear in the columns of the truth table.*

- *To simplify a tree structure, the data sub-sets subject to the actions are listed. The Boolean variables are ordered in each expression from left to right by frequency of appearance, with the most frequently used at the left. The skeleton of the tree structure thus emerges.*

- *When codes, identifies etc. . . . can take more than 2 values, they are converted into dummy binary codes. The dummy codes are noted in the data diagram and allow the truth tables to be compiled.*

EXERCISE

Take the following truth table for a data set E:

E								
A	B	C	D	V	W	X	Y	Z
0	0	0	0	X	X			
0	0	0	1	X	X			
0	0	1	0	X	X	X		X
0	0	1	1	X	X	X		
0	1	0	0	X				
0	1	0	1	X				
0	1	1	0	X				
0	1	1	1	X				
1	0	0	0				X	
1	0	0	1				X	
1	0	1	0				X	
1	0	1	1				X	
1	1	0	0	X				
1	1	0	1	X				
1	1	1	0	X				
1	1	1	1	X				

Construct the program to process the data set E.

SOLUTION

List of the data sets subject to the actions:

$V = B + \bar{B}.\bar{A}$

$W = \bar{B}.\bar{A}$

$X = \bar{B}.\bar{A}.C$

$Y = \bar{B}.A$

$Z = \bar{B}.\bar{A}.C.\bar{D}$

The action V must be programmed as a sub-routine which will be called twice (cf. Rule 3):

$$
\begin{aligned}
\text{1st call of SR V} &= B \\
\text{2nd call of SR V} &= \overline{B}.\overline{A}. \\
W &= \overline{B}.\overline{A} \\
X &= \overline{B}.\overline{A}.C \\
Z &= \overline{B}.\overline{A}.C.\overline{D} \\
Y &= \overline{B}.A
\end{aligned}
$$

Program set:

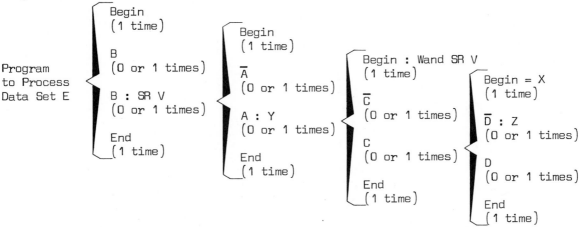

```
Program          ⎧ Begin
to Process       ⎪ (1 time)
Data Set E       ⎨
                 ⎪ B
                 ⎪ (0 or 1 times)
                 ⎪
                 ⎪ B : SR V
                 ⎪ (0 or 1 times)
                 ⎪
                 ⎪ End
                 ⎩ (1 time)

                        ⎧ Begin
                        ⎪ (1 time)
                        ⎨
                        ⎪ A̅
                        ⎪ (0 or 1 times)
                        ⎪
                        ⎪ A : Y
                        ⎪ (0 or 1 times)
                        ⎪
                        ⎪ End
                        ⎩ (1 time)

                               ⎧ Begin : Wand SR V
                               ⎪ (1 time)
                               ⎨
                               ⎪ C̅
                               ⎪ (0 or 1 times)
                               ⎪
                               ⎪ C
                               ⎪ (0 or 1 times)
                               ⎪
                               ⎪ End
                               ⎩ (1 time)

                                       ⎧ Begin = X
                                       ⎪ (1 time)
                                       ⎨
                                       ⎪ D̅ : Z
                                       ⎪ (0 or 1 times)
                                       ⎪
                                       ⎪ D
                                       ⎪ (0 or 1 times)
                                       ⎪
                                       ⎪ End
                                       ⎩ (1 time)
```

Note that this solution requires just 4 tests. Had the data sub-set subject to action V been defined as $\overline{A} + A.B$ then 5 tests would have been needed. To avoid this type of non-optimisation, use the Karnaugh Map where it is clear that action W coincides with the 2nd part of action V.

	$\overline{A}$	$\overline{A}$	A	A	
B	V	V	V	V	$\overline{D}$
B	V	V	V	V	
					D
$\overline{B}$	V W	V W X	Y	Y	
$\overline{B}$	V W	V W XZ	Y	Y	$\overline{D}$
	$\overline{C}$	C	C	$\overline{C}$	

This yields:

V (1st call) = B

V (2nd call) = $\overline{B}.\overline{A}$

W   = $\overline{B}.\overline{A}$ (coincides with V (2nd call))

    etc....

Whereas by defining $V = \overline{A} + A.B$

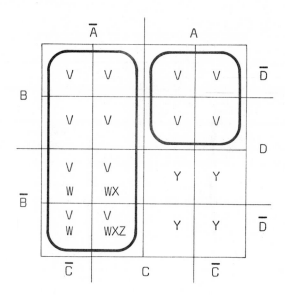

This yields:

V (1st call) = $\overline{A}$

V (2nd call) = A.B

W   = $\overline{A.B}$ (not coinciding with V (1st call) nor with V (2nd call), etc....

2 — COMPLEX ALTERNATIVE STRUCTURES IN PROGRAMS

A program constructed using a tree structure can be transformed into a complex alternative structure. To do this, an alternative is programmed for each action.

The solution using a complex alternative structure, although correct from the point of view of logic, is rarely the most economical in core memory space and above all in execution time. In this chapter rules are developed which help to determine whether to use the complex alternative structure or whether to use a composite solution.

Also the problems caused by the presence of several physical files of input data will be dealt with. The cases where a tree structure is the most suitable have already been seen.
An example already developed in the preceding chapter will be re-examined and it will be shown:

- how to construct a solution using a complex alternative structure,
- how to evaluate the benefit of this solution in comparison with that using a tree structure.

Example: The allocation of bonuses to the employees of an enterprise.
- Code A is used for employees having one year or more past service,
- Code B is used for management employees.

The truth table is as follows:

1 Employee A B	P_1	P_2	P_3	$\overline{R}$
0 0		X		
0 1				X
1 0			X	
1 1	X			

In a pure complex alternative structure, each simple alternative must include a null term. Thus, in this case, it is unnecessary to deal with $\overline{R}$ which is itself a set containing no processing. Consider the data sub-sets subject to the actions corresponding to bonuses P_1, P_2, P_3 :

$$P_1 \quad = \quad A.B$$
$$P_2 \quad = \quad \overline{A}.\overline{B}$$
$$P_3 \quad = \quad A.\overline{B}$$

The solution using a complex alternative structure is constructed as follows:

Employee
(E times)
{
Begin
(1 time)

P_1
(0 or 1 times)

φ
(0 or 1 times)

INT 1
(1 time)

P_2
(0 or 1 times)

φ
(0 or 1 times)

INT 2
(1 time)

P_3
(0 or 1 times)

φ
(0 or 1 times)

End
(1 time)

Flowchart:

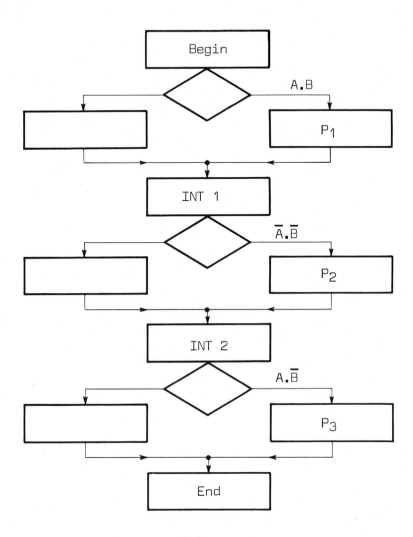

High-level languages allow each branch to be written as one instruction. However, each such branch will be compiled into 2 machine code instructions: (thus 'IF A AND B PERFORM P_1' represents *two* tests: that of A and that of B. Whereas in the tree structure for this example each branch corresponds to *one* test, that of A (or B)).

Here, the complex alternative solution demands in reality 6 tests instead of 3 in the other and the processing time is more than doubled. This is a special case: the tree structure is the natural choice, since all the data sub-sets subject to the actions are disjoint, but a complex alternative solution is nonetheless possible.

OPTIMAL SOLUTIONS USING COMPLEX ALTERNATIVE STRUCTURES

RULE

A program sub-set should be constructed by using a complex alternative structure if each of the data sub-sets subject to the actions intersects all of the others and provided that none of these intersections is an inclusion.

Example: The construction of an updating program for the products in the raw material stock of an enterprise.

The input data is a file sorted by product N° and containing for each product, in order, an old stock ('OS') record (0 or 1 times), a stock entry ('E') record (0 or 1 times) and a stock sent out ('S') record (0 or 1 times). For the results, a new stock ('NS') record is obtained for each product. Error conditions are ignored.

Processing: NS quantity = OS quantity + E quantity — S quantity.

Diagram of the results:

$$R \begin{cases} \text{Product} \\ \text{(P times)} \end{cases} \begin{cases} \text{NS} \ [\ + \ \text{QOS}, \ + \ \text{QE}, \ - \ \text{QS}\ ] \\ \text{(1 time)} \end{cases}$$

$$\bar{R} = \varphi$$

Diagram of the Input:

$$\text{Data} \begin{cases} \text{Product} \\ \text{(P times)} \end{cases} \begin{cases} \text{QS} \\ \text{(0 or 1 times)} \\ + \\ \text{E} \\ \text{(0 or 1 times)} \\ + \\ \text{S} \\ \text{(0 or 1 times)} \end{cases}$$

At the second level, the input data structure indicates that a truth table is required.

1 Product O E S	+QOS	+QE	−QS
0 0 0	φ	φ	φ
0 0 1	φ	φ	φ
0 1 0		X	
0 1 1		X	X
1 0 0	X		
1 0 1	X		X
1 1 0	X	X	
1 1 1	X	X	X

The number of alternatives at a certain level is equal to the number of mentioned variables. List of the data sub-sets subject to the actions:

+ QOS
+ QE
— QS

All these data sets intersect and there are no inclusions. The program is constructed using a complex alternative structure.

Here is the program subdivision:

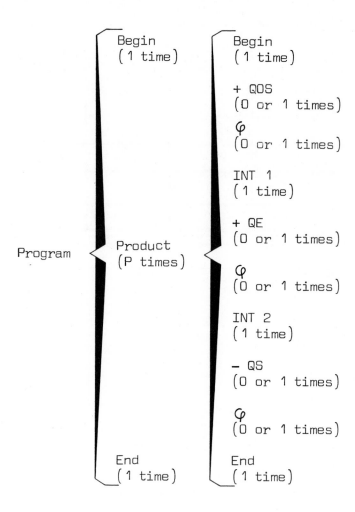

Flowchart:

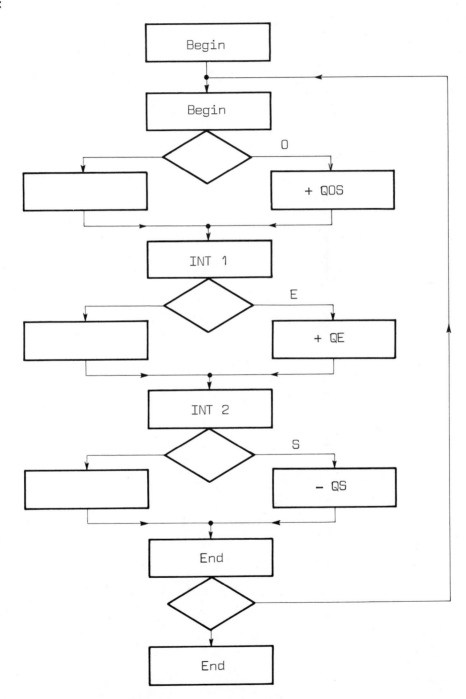

A solution using a tree structure is possible, but expensive, especially as regards core memory and sub-routine calls. Thus (SR = sub-routine call):

Program {

Product (P times) {

  Begin (1 time)

  $\overline{O}$ (0 or 1 times) {
    Begin SR + QE (1 time)
    $\overline{S}$ (0 or 1 times)
    S SR − QS (0 or 1 times)
    End (1 time)
  }

  O (0 or 1 times) {

    $\overline{\overline{E}}$ (0 or 1 times) {
      Begin (1 time)
      Begin (1 time)
      $\overline{S}$ (0 or 1 times)
      S SR − QS (0 or 1 times)
      End (1 time)
    }

    E (0 or 1 times) {
      Begin (1 time)
      Begin SR + QE (1 time)
      $\overline{S}$ (0 or 1 times)
      S SR − QS (0 or 1 times)
      End (1 time)
    }

    End (1 time)
  }

  End (1 time)
}

End (1 time)
}

It is unnecessary to distinguish $\overline{O}.\overline{E}$ and $\overline{O}.E$ since by convention (error conditions ignored) within the set $\overline{O}$ the sub-set $\overline{O}.\overline{E}$ is null (i.e. if there is no Old Stock, there must always be an Entry).

Table to compare the two solutions as regards the number of tests and sub-routine calls:

Solution	Tests	Sub-routine calls
Tree structure	5	5
Complex alternative structure	3	0

This example, in contrast with that preceding, shows the advantages of complex alternative structures in certain cases, here fewer instructions to write since the data sub-sets to the actions all intersect with no inclusions. Moreover, it is possible to simplify the Boolean expression of the data sub-sets (i.e. because $\overline{O}.\overline{E} = \emptyset$).

MULTIPLE SOURCES OF INPUT

When the input data are divided between several physical files, the program construction can be affected if the files are sequential and if no single file can be used as a master (guide) file.
First of all the hierarchical structure of the input data will be dealt with.

Example: Take the stock updating example. The problem statement is modified in the following respects: there are 3 physical input files:

- Old stock OS (0 or 1 records per product)
- Stock Entry E (0 or 1 records per product)
- Stock Sent out S (0 or 1 records per product)

Run diagram:

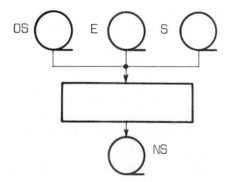

In each file, the records are sorted in ascending order on the product N°. The diagram of the input data is represented by:

$$
\text{Data}
\left\{
\begin{array}{l}
\text{Product} \\
\text{(P times)}
\end{array}
\right.
\left\{
\begin{array}{l}
\text{OS} \\
\text{(0 or 1 times)} \\
+ \\
\text{E} \\
\text{(0 or 1 times)} \\
+ \\
\text{S} \\
\text{(0 or 1 times)}
\end{array}
\right.
$$

Thus the diagram of the input data is identical with that obtained when there is only one physical file: the data are the same in both cases. However, the construction of the program poses a few problems. Indeed, for each file, there is an input area containing the next record to process for the file in question. Since there are 3 such records, the N° of the next product to process is unknown and it must above all be determined.

RULE

Before processing a data set, the reference criterion allowing the elements of the set to be identified must be determined and stored in core memory.

To execute a test, the two terms of the comparison must be available. These two terms are items of information:

- THE REFERENCE CRITERION is the term against which the comparison is made and which is mentioned in the above rule. The reference criterion must be saved during the time required for processing all the elements of the data set.
- THE IDENTIFICATION CRITERION is the term which is compared. Each element of data must be accompanied by its identification criterion in order to be processed.

In the stock example, the reference criterion is not automically known; it must be determined. Since the data are sorted by ascending order on the product N°, the N° of the product to process is the smallest N° of the three available in the three input areas of core memory.

The reference criterion is obtained by a series of comparisons. The identification (product N°) of the first file is compared with that of the second and the smaller is stored in a reference field (RF). The identification criterion of the third file is then compared with that in the reference field. If the identifier of the third file is the smaller it is transferred to the reference field, if not, no transfer takes place. The reference field finally contains the reference criterion.

Thus a series of comparisons is performed to determine the reference criterion of a set whose elements come from several physical files, of which none can be relied upon to supply the reference criterion. This implies a string of alternative structures in the program set. The number of alternatives will be equal to the number of files minus one.

In the stock example, here is the organisation of the program as regards the determination of the reference criterion for each product.

Diagram of the program sub-set:

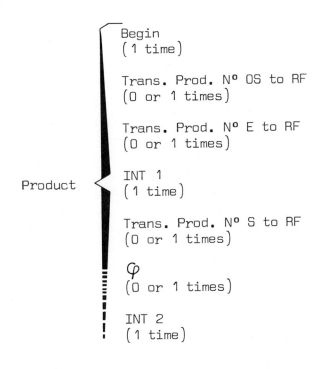

Product

Begin
(1 time)

Trans. Prod. N° OS to RF
(0 or 1 times)

Trans. Prod. N° E to RF
(0 or 1 times)

INT 1
(1 time)

Trans. Prod. N° S to RF
(0 or 1 times)

φ
(0 or 1 times)

INT 2
(1 time)

Flowchart:

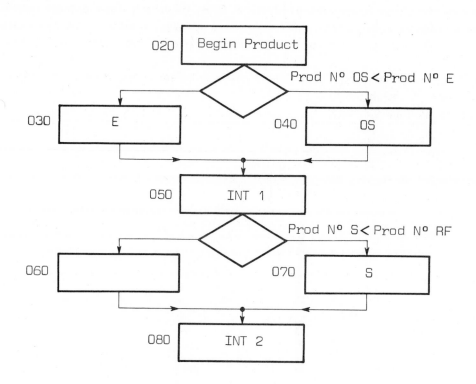

Here is the detailed organisation of this part of the program:

SEQUENCES	INSTRUCTIONS	NEXT SEQUENCE
020 Begin Product	Process Begin Product	
	IF Prod. N° OS< Prod. N° E	040
030	Trans. Prod. N° E to RF	050
040	Trans. Prod. N° OS to RF	
050 INT 1	If Prod. N° S< Prod. N° RF	070
060	....	080
070	Trans. Prod. N° S to RF	
080 INT 2	....	

Generally speaking, when there are several input files, the presence of any record from any file should always be considered as random. Indeed, even if records must be present on one of the files (master or guide), the error condition arising when they are in fact absent should always be provided for.

RULE

When there are several physical input files and when none of them can be used as a guide file, the reference criterion of each set to process must be determined before starting the processing. This is done by a series of comparisons in order to transfer the smallest key to a reference field if the processing is by ascending order of keys as is usual. (If this is not the case, the modifications required are obvious.)

Normally the number of comparisons is equal to the number of files minus one.

COMPOSITE SOLUTIONS

Definition: A composite solution is one where the program is constructed from the truth table partly by using a tree structure and partly by using a complex alternative structure.

The number of combinations than can be met with when developing composite solutions is practically unlimited.

RULE

A composite solution can be sought whenever the data sets subject to the actions noted on the table are partly disjoint or wholly included and partly not (i.e. whenever a pure tree or complex alternative structure cannot be used).

Example: Take a table for a set D of data including three non-exclusive sub-sets A, B and C and five actions V, W, X, Y and Z:

D A B C	V	W	X	Y	Z
0 0 0	X				
0 0 1	X		X		
0 1 0				X	
0 1 1			X	X	
1 0 0		X			
1 0 1		X	X		X
1 1 0		X			
1 1 1		X	X		X

List of the data sub-sets subject to the different actions:

$V = \overline{A}.\overline{B}$

$W = A$

$X = C$

$Y = \overline{A}.B$

$Z = A.C$

The following grouping of sets that are disjoint or included can be made:

- first group: $V = \overline{A}.\overline{B}.$

                        $W = A$

                        $Y = \overline{A}.B$

                        $Z = A.C$
- second group: $X = C$

This grouping leads to a complex alternative structure where one alternative is developed using a tree structure for actions V, W, Y and Z. The other alternative will be used for action X. Here is the corresponding program sub-division:

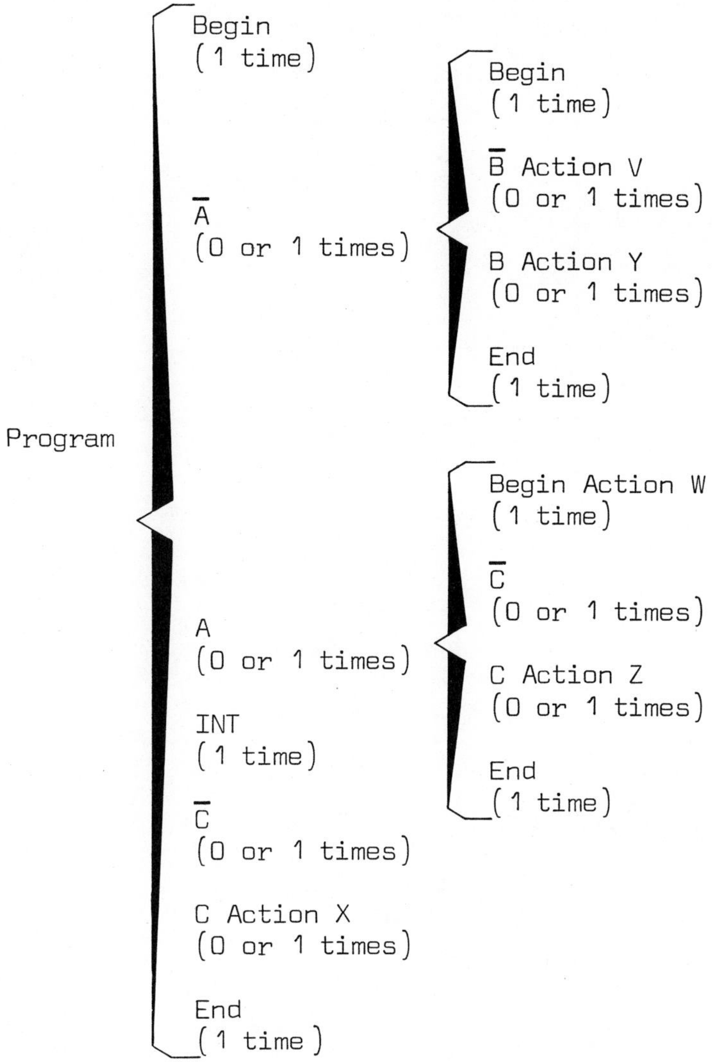

Program

Begin
(1 time)

$\overline{A}$
(0 or 1 times)

Begin
(1 time)

$\overline{B}$ Action V
(0 or 1 times)

B Action Y
(0 or 1 times)

End
(1 time)

A
(0 or 1 times)

Begin Action W
(1 time)

$\overline{C}$
(0 or 1 times)

C Action Z
(0 or 1 times)

End
(1 time)

INT
(1 time)

$\overline{C}$
(0 or 1 times)

C Action X
(0 or 1 times)

End
(1 time)

Flowchart:

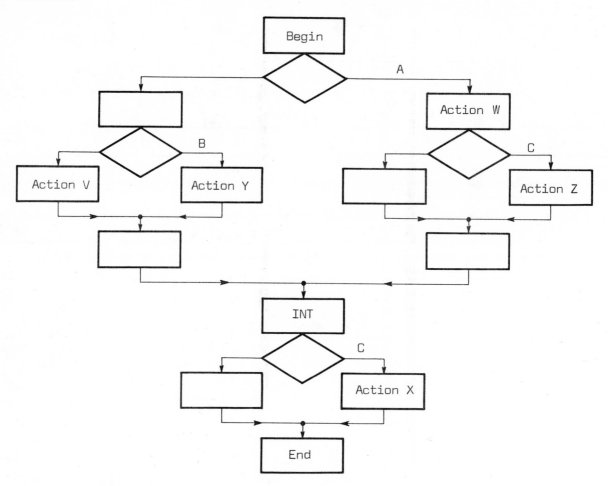

A second solution can be obtained by the following grouping:

- first group: $V = \overline{A}.\overline{B}$
                    $Y = \overline{A}.B$
                    $W = A$
- second group: $X = C$
                    $Z = C.A$

This leads to another composite solution:

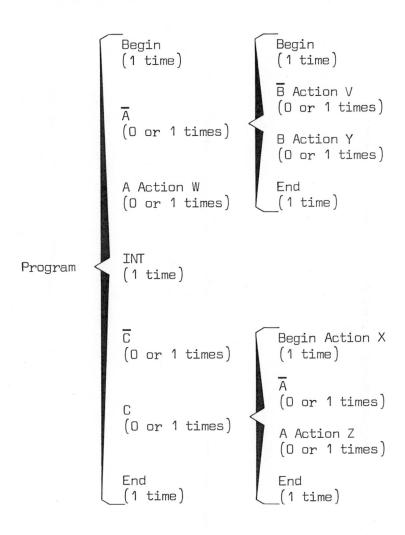

The solution using a tree structure would be:

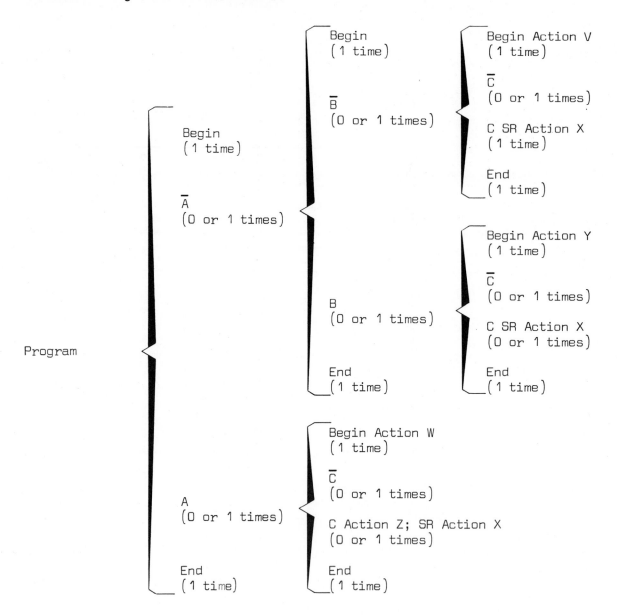

The different solutions will be compared as regards core memory occupation (number of instructions written: tests and sub-routine calls) and performance (average number of instructions executed during a run).

Solution	Memory Occupation		Instructions per Run	
	Tests	SR Calls	Tests	SR Calls
1 st Composite	4	0	3	0
2 nd Composite	4	0	3	0
Tree	5	3	2,5	0,5
Complex Alternative	8	0	8	0

Thus it can be seen that composite solutions generally reduce memory occupation and processing time. This example shows a composite solution whose highest level is a complex alternative structure. There are in fact two types of composite solution:

- Those whose highest level is a complex alternative i.e. none of the Boolean variables are present in all the expressions.

- Those whose highest level is the root of a tree i.e. one, at least, of the Boolean variables is present in all the expressions.

Here is an example of a solution in the second category:

D			V	W	X	Y	Z
A	B	C					
0	0	0		X			
0	0	1		X			
0	1	0	X			X	X
0	1	1	X		X		X
1	0	0		X			
1	0	1		X			
1	1	0	X			X	
1	1	1	X		X		

List of the data sub-sets subject to the actions:

$$V = B$$
$$W = \bar{B}$$
$$X = B.C$$
$$Y = B.\bar{C}$$
$$Z = B.\bar{A}$$

The variable B is present in all the expressions: thus at the highest level, a tree structure whose root is B is used.

At the first level, the program can be represented:

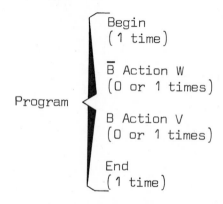

Program
- Begin (1 time)
- $\bar{B}$ Action W (0 or 1 times)
- B Action V (0 or 1 times)
- End (1 time)

In the program set B, action V is always executed. The remaining actions are to be performed upon sub-sets of B:

$$X = C$$
$$Y = \overline{C}$$
$$Z = \overline{A}$$

At this level, a complex alternative must be used, one of whose modules is developed into a tree structure with 2 terms. Here is the diagram:

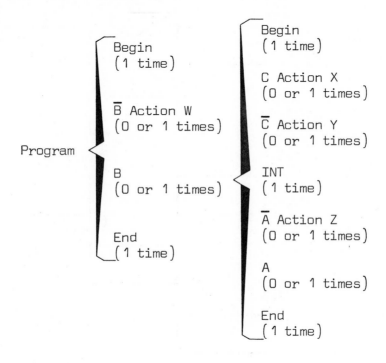

Program

Begin
(1 time)

$\overline{B}$ Action W
(0 or 1 times)

B
(0 or 1 times)

End
(1 time)

Begin
(1 time)

C Action X
(0 or 1 times)

$\overline{C}$ Action Y
(0 or 1 times)

INT
(1 time)

$\overline{A}$ Action Z
(0 or 1 times)

A
(0 or 1 times)

End
(1 time)

Flowchart:

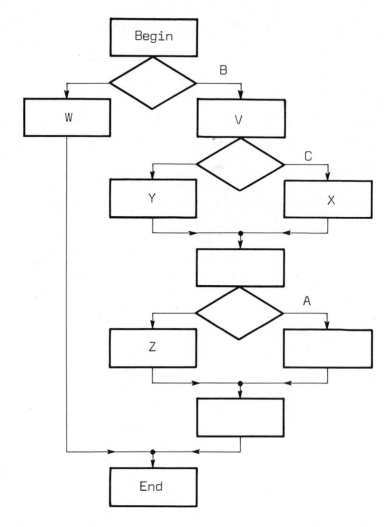

Here is the table comparing the composite, tree structure and complex alternative solutions:

Solution	Memory Occupation		Instructions per RVN	
	Tests	SR Calls	Tests	SR Calls
Composite	3	0	2	0
Tree	4	2	2	0,5
Complex Alternative	8	0	8	0

It can be observed that, by using a composite solution, the gain in processing time goes hand in hand with the gain in memory space.

Before leaving composite solutions the case of multiple sources of input in a tree structure must be reviewed.

RULE

Whenever there are multiple sources of input in a tree structure, the input instruction corresponding to the root of the tree is located in the appropriate sequence. The input instructions for the other files are located in alternatives programmed in the set after the actual processing with one alternative for each file.

This solution appears to be the most economical while at the same time being the most sure, since the programmer does not run the risk of forgetting an input instruction.

Example: Take the following tree structure with 2 physical files A and B. Here is the flowchart with the read (input) instructions shown:

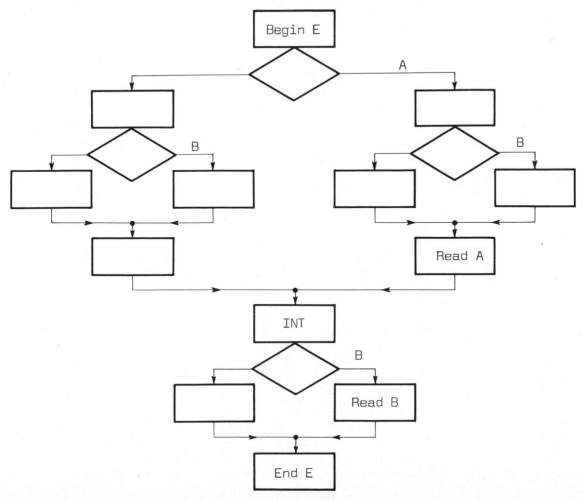

Without the alternative for the reading of file B, the flowchart would have been:

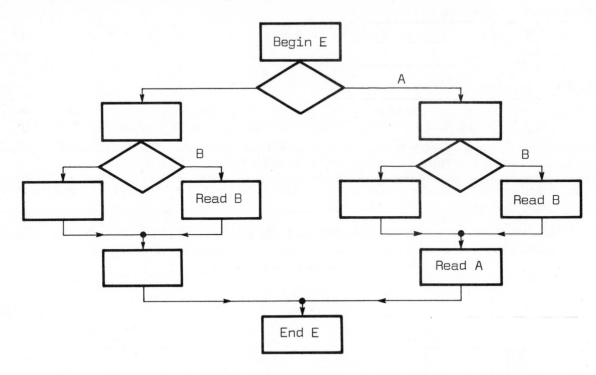

In any case, note that read instructions are better managed by using sub-routines. The standard sub-routine for input which will allow the file to be 'read' after detecting the end of file record is:

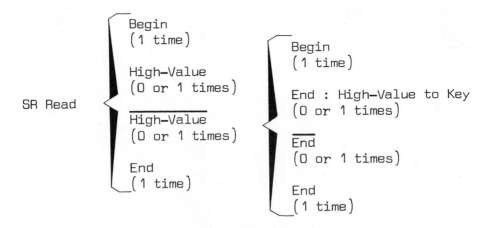

RECAPITULATIVE EXAMPLE

From 4 files, sorted by product N°, periodically the following files must be obtained:

- a file of goods unsold during the previous period,
- a file of unvalued deliveries,
- a file of valued packing,
- a report of valued deliveries,
- an error file of product N^{os} lacking a description record.

Run diagram:

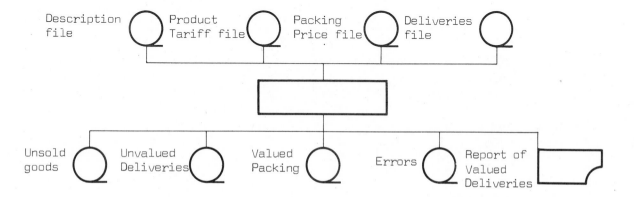

Input data:

- Description file (0 or 1 records per product: if zero error condition):

Product N°	Descr.

- Product tariff (0 or 1 records per product)

Product N°	Unit Price

- Deliveries (0 or 1 records per product)

Product N°	Quantity

- Packing price (0 or 1 records per product)

Product N°	Packing Price

The product N° shows both the product and the type of packing if any; the same product will have several different Product N°s according to the packing used. The unvalued deliveries correspond to products with no tariff; these products can, however, have packing that is to be paid for.

The results:

- Unsold goods (0 or 1 records per product)

Product N°

- Unvalued deliveries (0 or 1 records per product)

Product N°	Quantity

- Valued packing (0 or 1 records per product)

Product N°	Packing Price	Quantity	Value

- Errors (0 or 1 records per product)

Product N°

- Report of valued deliveries (0 or 1 lines per product)

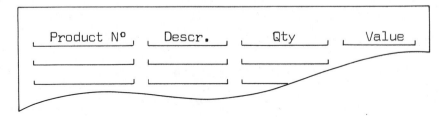

Diagram of the results:

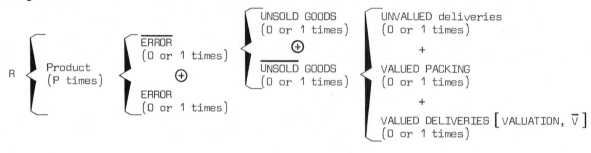

$$\bar{R} = \varphi$$

Diagram of the input data:

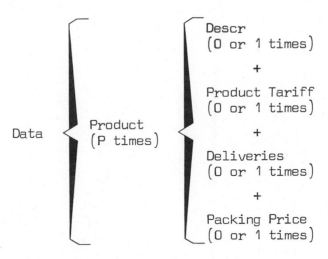

At the first level, the program will be repetitive. At the second, the reference criterion must be determined by alternatives before starting the actual processing. After the processing will be the alternatives for the read instructions.

The actual processing involves the drawing up of a table. However, to simplify documentation, the universal set can be taken as 1 product delivered since the set of undelivered products corresponds to the error processing. This will cut the table to half its size (8 minterms instead of 16). The first 2 levels of the program are:

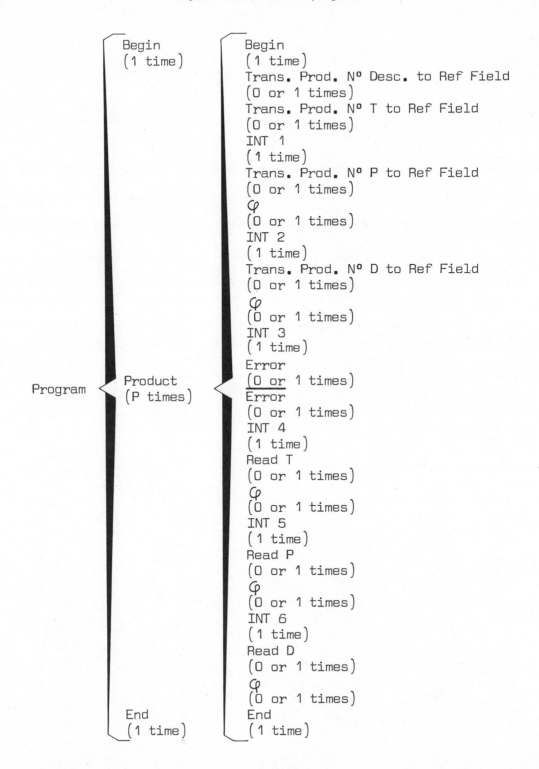

Truth table for 1 product delivered (Packing price = P; Product Tariff = T; Delivery = D):

1 Delivery P T D	Unsold Goods	Unvalued Deliveries	Valued Packing	Report of Deliveries	Valuation
0 0 0	X				
0 0 1		X		X	
0 1 0	X				
0 1 1				X	X
1 0 0	X				
1 0 1		X	X	X	
1 1 0	X				
1 1 1			X	X	X

List of the data sub-sets subject to the actions:

Unsold	=	$\overline{D}$
Unvalued Deliveries	=	$D.\overline{T}$
Valued Packing	=	$D.P$
Report	=	D
Valuation	=	$D.T$

At the first level of processing a tree structure is used: the variable D which is present in all the expressions is the root.
In the set of products delivered, there remain the sub-sets:

Unvalued deliveries	=	$\overline{T}$
Valued Packing	=	P
Valuation	=	T

This last level is constructed using a composite solution: the first alternative is a tree (test T) and the second processes the packing (test P).

Here is the complete diagram for the program:

```
                    ┌ Begin          ┌ Begin
                    │ (1 time)       │ (1 time)
                    │                │ Trans. Prod. Nº Desc. to Ref Field
                    │                │ (0 or 1 times)
                    │                │ Trans. Prod. Nº T to Ref Field
                    │                │ (0 or 1 times)
                    │                │ INT 1
                    │                │ (1 time)
                    │                │ Trans. Prod. Nº P to Ref Field
                    │                │ (0 or 1 times)
                    │                │ φ
                    │                │ (0 or 1 times)
                    │                │ INT 2
                    │                │ (1 time)
                    │                │ Trans. Prod. Nº D to ref Field
                    │                │ (0 or 1 times)
                    │                │ φ
                    │                │ (0 or 1 times)                                          ┌ Begin
                    │                │ INT 3                                                   │ (1 time)
                    │                │ (1 time)                         ┌ Begin               │ T Valuation
                    │                │ Error                            │ (1 time)            │ (0 or 1 times)
          ┌ Product │                │ (0 or 1 times)                   │ D Unsold            │ T Unvalued deliveries
Program ⟨ │ (P      ⟨                ⟨ Error                            ⟨ (0 or 1 times)      │ (0 or 1 times)
          │  times) │                │ (0 or 1 times)                   │ D                   │ INT 10
                    │                │ INT 4                            │ (0 or 1 times)    ⟨ │ (1 time)
                    │                │ (1 time)                         │ End                 │ P Valued packing
                    │                │ Read T                           └ (1 time)            │ (0 or 1 times)
                    │                │ (0 or 1 times)                                          │ P̄
                    │                │ φ                                                       │ (0 or 1 times)
                    │                │ (0 or 1 times)                                          │ End
                    │                │ INT 5                                                   └ (1 time)
                    │                │ (1 time)
                    │                │ Read P
                    │                │ (0 or 1 times)
                    │                │ φ
                    │                │ (0 or 1 times)
                    │                │ INT 6
                    │                │ (1 time)
                    │                │ Read D
                    │                │ (0 or 1 times)
                    │                │ φ
                    │ End            │ (0 or 1 times)
                    │ (1 time)       │ End
                    └                └ (1 time)
```

Flowchart:

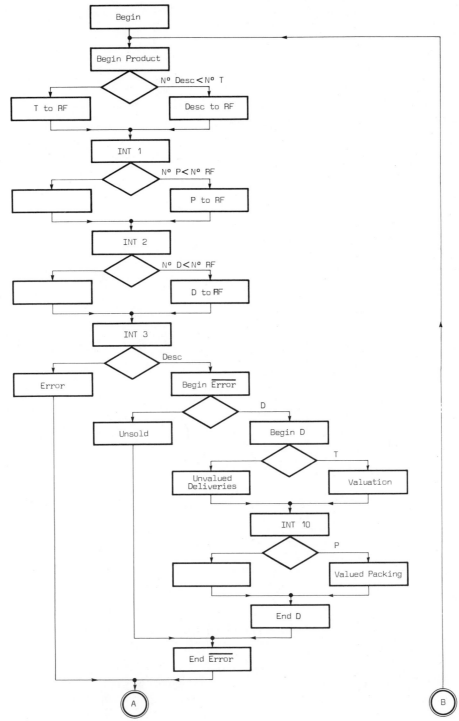

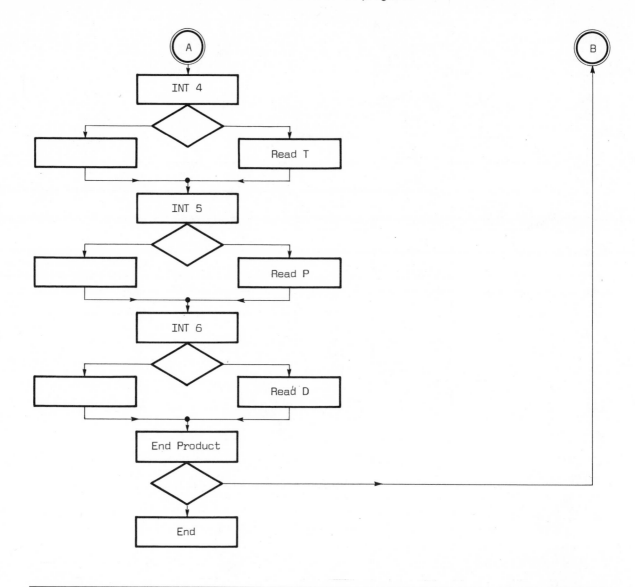

SUMMARY

- *Any program can be constructed using complex alternative structures, but this solution has rarely the best performance.*

- *A program sub-set is constructed with a complex alternative structure when each of the data sub-sets subject to the actions intersects with all the others and provided that none of these intersections is an inclusion.*

- *Before processing a data set, the reference criterion allowing the elements of the set to be identified must be determined and stored in core memory. When there are several physical input files, this criterion is sought by a series of comparisons.*

- *Whenever there are multiple sources of input in a tree structure, the input (read) instruction corresponding to the root of the tree is located in the appropriate sequence. The input instructions for the other files are located in alternatives programmed in the set after the actual processing with one alternative for each file.*

- *A composite solution (partly tree, partly complex alternative) must be sought whenever pure solutions cannot be used i.e. When the data sets subject to the actions are partly disjoint or wholly included and partly not.*

EXERCISE

A London firm requires:
- a monthly report of sales by product
- a file of unsold products
- a file of those product numbers for which an error has been encountered

RUN DIAGRAM

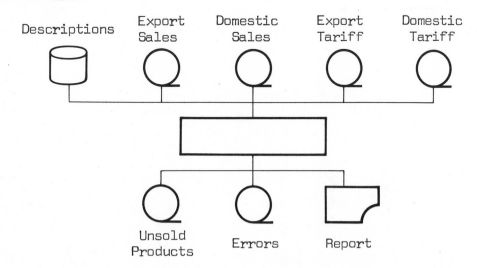

RESULTS

Report: 0 or 1 lines per product, 0 if errors.

Product N°	Description	Total Quantity	Domestic Value	Export Value

			Total Domestic Value	Total Export Value

Total Quantity = Export Quantity + Domestic Quantity

Domestic (Export) Value = Domestic (Export) Quantity × Domestic (Export) Tariff.

The Domestic (Export) Value is the amount of money generated by Domestic (Export) Sales for each product valued by the Domestic (Export) tariff expressed in local (international) currency.

Errors: 0 or 1 records per product, 1 if error.

Product N°	Text Describing Error

Unsold products: 0 or 1 records per product, 1 if the product has not been sold during the month and if there are no errors.

Product N°	Description

DATA

Description file (D): 0 or 1 records per product. If there is no record for a supposedly existing product, then this is an error.

Product N°	Description

Export sales (ES): 0 or 1 records per product.

Product N°	Quantity

Domestic sales (DS): 0 or 1 records per product.

| Product Nº | Quantity |

Export Tariff (ET): 0 or 1 records per product. If there is no record for a supposedly existing product number, then this is an error.

| Product Nº | Export Tariff |

Domestic Tariff (DT): 0 or 1 records per product. If there is no record for a supposedly existing product number, then this is an error.

| Product Nº | Domestic Tariff |

PROCESSING

Calculations:

- Total Quantity = Export Quantity + Domestic Quantity
- Domestic Value = Domestic Quantity × Domestic Tariff
- Export Value = Export Quantity × Export Tariff
- Accumulate Domestic Values giving Total Domestic Value
- Accumulate Export Values giving Total Export Value

Error conditions:
- no Description   record for a supposedly existing product ($\overline{D}$)
- no Export tariff   „   „ „   „   „   „   ($\overline{ET}$)
- no Domestic tariff „   „ „   „   „   „   ($\overline{DT}$)

Do the solution up to the program subdivision into logical sequences and then compare your solution with that illustrated in the pages that follow.

SOLUTION

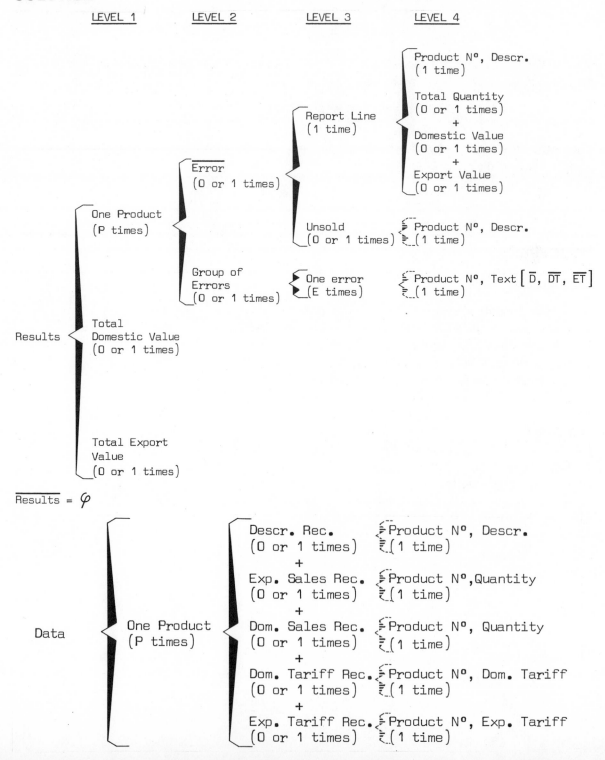

LEVEL 1   LEVEL 2   LEVEL 3   LEVEL 4

Product Nº, Descr.
(1 time)

Total Quantity
(0 or 1 times)
+
Domestic Value
(0 or 1 times)
+
Export Value
(0 or 1 times)

Report Line
(1 time)

Error
(0 or 1 times)

Unsold
(0 or 1 times)   Product Nº, Descr.
(1 time)

One Product
(P times)

Group of
Errors
(0 or 1 times)   One error
(E times)   Product Nº, Text $[\overline{D}, \overline{DT}, \overline{ET}]$
(1 time)

Results

Total
Domestic Value
(0 or 1 times)

Total Export
Value
(0 or 1 times)

$\overline{\text{Results}} = \varphi$

Descr. Rec.
(0 or 1 times)   Product Nº, Descr.
(1 time)
+
Exp. Sales Rec.
(0 or 1 times)   Product Nº, Quantity
(1 time)
+
Data   One Product
(P times)   Dom. Sales Rec.
(0 or 1 times)   Product Nº, Quantity
(1 time)
+
Dom. Tariff Rec.
(0 or 1 times)   Product Nº, Dom. Tariff
(1 time)
+
Exp. Tariff Rec.
(0 or 1 times)   Product Nº, Exp. Tariff
(1 time)

Program diagram: Truth table for 1 product:

	ONE PRODUCT					ERR. $\overline{D}$	ERR. $\overline{ET}$	ERR. $\overline{DT}$	Write ERR.	Write Unsold	Print Line	Calc. Exp. Val.	Calc. Dom. Val.
	D	ES	DS	ET	DT								
0	0	0	0	0	0	φ	φ	φ	φ	φ	φ	φ	φ
1	0	0	0	0	1	X	X		X				
2	0	0	0	1	0	X		X	X				
3	0	0	0	1	1	X			X				
4	0	0	1	0	0	X	X	X	X				
5	0	0	1	0	1	X	X		X				
6	0	0	1	1	0	X		X	X				
7	0	0	1	1	1	X			X				
8	0	1	0	0	0	X	X	X	X				
9	0	1	0	0	1	X	X		X				
10	0	1	0	1	0	X		X	X				
11	0	1	0	1	1	X			X				
12	0	1	1	0	0	X	X	X	X				
13	0	1	1	0	1	X	X		X				
14	0	1	1	1	0	X		X	X				
15	0	1	1	1	1	X			X				
16	1	0	0	0	0		X	X	X				
17	1	0	0	0	1		X		X				
18	1	0	0	1	0			X	X				
19	1	0	0	1	1					X	X		
20	1	0	1	0	0		X	X	X				
21	1	0	1	0	1		X		X				
22	1	0	1	1	0			X	X				
23	1	0	1	1	1						X		X
24	1	1	0	0	0		X	X	X				
25	1	1	0	0	1		X		X				
26	1	1	0	1	0			X	X				
27	1	1	0	1	1						X	X	
28	1	1	1	0	0		X	X	X				
29	1	1	1	0	1		X		X				
30	1	1	1	1	0			X	X				
31	1	1	1	1	1						X	X	X

D = Descr.	ERR. $\overline{D}$ = $\overline{D}$	Print line = D.ET.DT
ES = Exp. Sales	ERR. $\overline{ET}$ = $\overline{ET}$	Calc. Exp. Val. = D.ET.DT.ES
DS = Dom. Sales	ERR. $\overline{DT}$ = $\overline{DT}$	Calc. Dom. Val. = D.ET.DT.DS
ET = Exp. Tariff	Write Err. = $\overline{D} + \overline{ET} + \overline{DT}$	
DT = Dom. Tariff	Write Unsold = D.ET.DT.$\overline{ES}$.$\overline{DS}$	

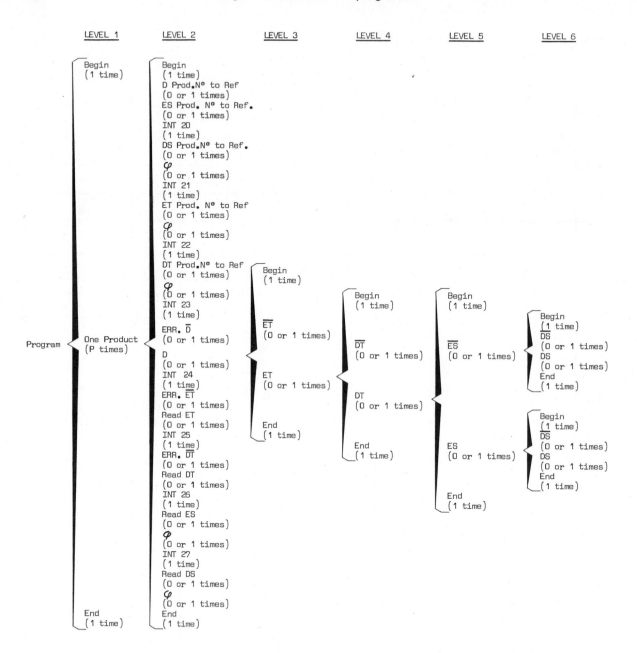

**Flowchart
up to level 2:**

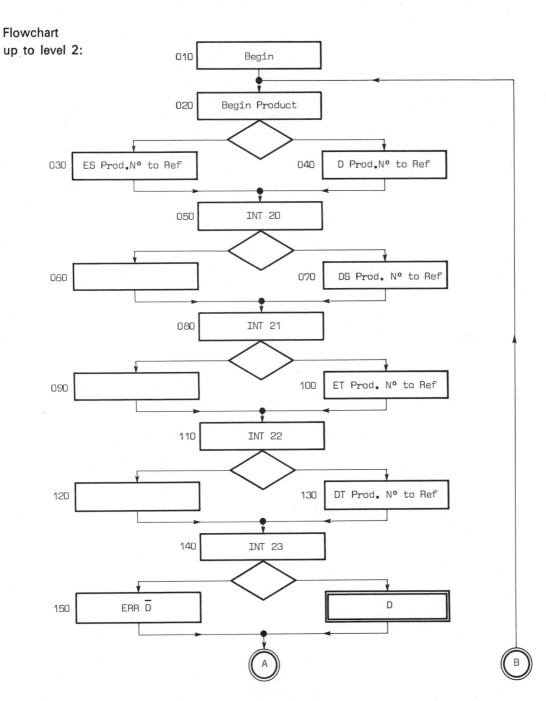

010	Begin
020	Begin Product
030	ES Prod. Nº to Ref
040	D Prod. Nº to Ref
050	INT 20
060	
070	DS Prod. Nº to Ref
080	INT 21
090	
100	ET Prod. Nº to Ref
110	INT 22
120	
130	DT Prod. Nº to Ref
140	INT 23
150	ERR D̄ / D

Note that the Read instructions for Exp. Tariff and Dom. Tariff have been programmed in the same alternative structures as the corresponding error conditions (sequences 340 and 370).

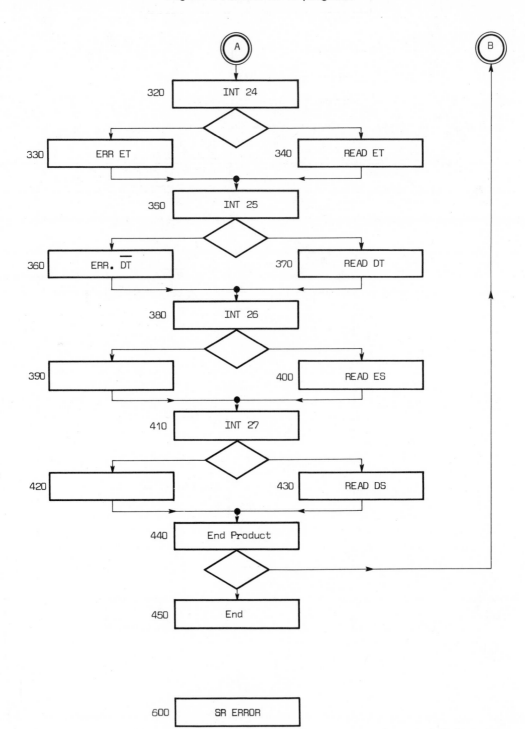

Flowchart for the sub-set D:

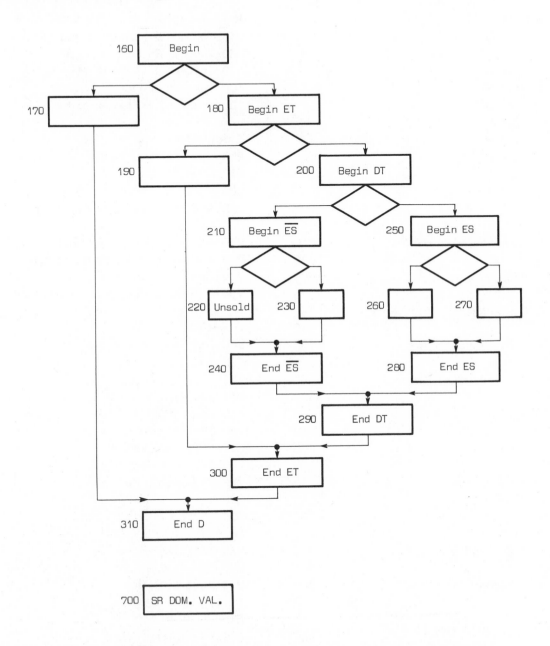

Now do the detailed organisation and then compare your solution with that outlined in the following pages:

Detailed organisation : Instruction Lists by Type

Read
010 Read D
010 Read ES
010 Read DS
010 Read ET
010 Read DT
310 Read D
340 Read ET
370 Read DT
400 Read ES
430 Read DS

Branch

020 If D Prod N° < ES Prod N°	040	
030	050	
050 If DS Prod N° < Ref	070	
060	080	
080 If ET Prod N° < Ref	100	
090	110	
110 If DT Prod N° < Ref	130	
120	140	
140 If D Prod N° = Ref	160	
150	320	
160 If ET Prod N° = Ref	180	
170	310	
180 If DT Prod N° = Ref	200	
190	300	
200 If ES Prod N° = Ref	250	
210 If DS Prod N° = Ref	230	
220	240	
240	290	
250 If DS Prod N° = Ref	270	
260	280	
320 If ET Prod N° = Ref	340	
330	350	
350 If DT Prod N° = Ref	370	
360	380	
380 If ES Prod N° = Ref	400	
390	410	
410 If DS Prod N° = Ref	430	
420	440	
440 If $\overline{EOF}$ (all files)	020	

Preparation of Branch
040 Transfer D Prod N° to Ref
030 Transfer ES Prod N° to Ref.
070 Transfer DS Prod N° to Ref.
100 Transfer ET Prod N° to Ref.
130 Transfer DT Prod N° to Ref.

Calculations
010 Clear Tot. Exp. Value
010 Clear Tot. Dom. Value
200 Clear Tot. Quantity
250 Add ES Quantity to Tot. Quantity
250 Calc. Exp. Value
250 Add Exp. Value to Tot. Value
700 Add Dom Sales Qty to Tot. Qty
700 Calc. Dom. Value
700 Add Dom. Value to Tot. Dom. Value

Outputs
200 Edit Prod. N° and Descr.
290 Edit Tot. Quantity
250 Edit Exp. Value
700 Edit Dom. Value
450 Edit Tot. Dom. Value
450 Edit Tot. Exp. Value
290 Print and Restore line
450 Print and Restore line
220 Edit Unsold Rec
220 Write Unsold Rec.
150 Edit. ERR. $\overline{D}$
360 Edit. ERR. $\overline{DT}$
330 Edit. ERR. $\overline{ET}$
600 Edit Prod N°
600 Write ERR. Rec.

Sub-routine calls
150 SR ERROR
360 SR ERROR
330 SR ERROR
230 SR DOM. VAL.
270 SR DOM. VAL.

Detailed organisation : Sorted Instruction List

010	Read D	
	Read ES	
	Read DS	
	Read ET	
	Read DT	
	Clear Tot. Exp. Val.	
	Clear Tot. Dom. Val.	
020	If D Prod N° < ES Prod N°	040
030	Transf. ES Prod N° to Ref	050
040	Transf. D Prod N° to Ref	
050	If DS Prod N° < Ref	070
060		080
070	Trans. DS Prod N° to Ref	
080	If ET Prod N° < Ref	100
090		110
100	Transf. ET Prod N° to Ref	
110	If DT Prod N° < Ref.	130
120		140
130	Transf. DT Prod N° to Ref	
140	If D Prod N° = Ref	160
150	Edit ERR. $\bar{D}$	
	Call SR ERROR	320
160	If ET Prod N° = Ref	180
170		310
180	If DT Prod N° = Ref	200
190		300
200	Clear Tot. Quantity	
	Edit. Prod N° and Descr.	
	If ES Prod N° = Ref	250
210	If DS Prod N° = Ref	230
220	Edit Unsold Rec.	
	Write Unsold Rec.	240
230	Call SR DOM. VAL	
240		290
250	Add ES Qty to Tot. Qty	
	Calc. Exp. Value	
	Add. Exp. Value to Tot. Exp. Val.	

	Edit Exp. Value	
	If DS Prod N° = Ref	270
260		280
270	Call SR DOM. VAL.	
280		
290	Edit Total Qty	
	Print and Restore line	
300		
310	Read D	
320	If ET Prod N° = Ref	340
330	Edit ERR. $\overline{ET}$	
	Call SR ERROR	350
340	Read ET	
350	If DT Prod N° = Ref	370
360	Edit ERR $\overline{DT}$	
	Call SR ERROR	380
370	Read DT	
380	If ES Prod N° = Ref	400
390		410
400	Read ES	
410	If DS Prod N° = Ref	430
420		
430	Read DS	
440	If $\overline{EOF}$ (all files)	020
450	Edit Tot. Exp. Val.	
	Edit Tot. Dom. Val.	
	Print and Restore line	

SR ERROR
600 Edit Prod N°
     Write Err. Rec.

SR DOM. VAL.
700 Add DS Qty to Tot. Qty
     Calc. Dom. Value
     Add Dom. Val. to Tot. Dom. Val.
     Edit Dom. Val.

3 — CHAIN-LINKED TRUTH TABLES

CHAINS OF TABLES

RULE

Truth tables must be compiled for each complex alternative structure of the input data. When such structures occur at several consecutive levels, the tables at higher levels transfer to the tables at lower levels. These transfers generate what is called the chain-linking of tables.

Once again, the advantages of the hierarchical approach are apparent, since it is easy to construct a program from several relatively small tables. Indeed, the use of tables for more than 6 sets is very difficult in practice and the Karnaugh map becomes unwieldy. When the hierarchical approach is not used, tables that are too large are split arbitrarily, thus opportunities for program optimisation are nearly always overlooked.

When tables occur at 2 consecutive levels, the table at the higher level transfers to the tables at the lower level.

In order to complete the results diagram, the data sets subject to the actions producing output must be identified. In this way the actions can be noted in the tables correctly.
Example: Take the following data set:

This example concerns the calculation of a bonus for the employees of an enterprise. The symbols are used with the meanings:

- Emp for an employee
- P   for a record of the personnel file
- A   for a record of the permanent employees files
        ($\bar{A}$: temporary personnel)
- B   for a record of the file of employees paid by the hour
        ($\bar{B}$: those paid monthly).

Thus, a temporary employee paid monthly will have a record on file P but no record on files A and B. C, D and E are values of a code used in records from file B:

- C for foremen
- D for employees doing dangerous work
- E for employees who work away from their home town.

Thus $\bar{C}$ means the ordinary workers (those not foremen), $\bar{D}$ the employees not doing dangerous work and $\bar{E}$ those working in their home town.

The ruling of the allocation of a bonus will be:

— Annual bonus of V for all employees paid monthly ($\bar{B}$)
— Monthly bonus for the other employees (B) as follows:
  - W, calculated by:
    formula a for temporary workers (B.$\bar{A}$.$\bar{C}$.)
    and formula b for temporary foremen (B.$\bar{A}$.C.)
  - X, calculated by:
    formula c for temporary workers doing dangerous work (B.$\bar{A}$.$\bar{C}$.D.)
    and formula d for permanent workers doing dangerous work (B.A.$\bar{C}$.D)
  - Y, calculated by:
    formula e for temporary workers working away from their home town (B.$\bar{A}$.$\bar{C}$.E)
    and formula f for permanent workers working in their home town (B.A.$\bar{C}$.$\bar{E}$)
  - Z, calculated by:
    formula g for permanent foremen (B.A.C)
    and formula h for workers not doing dangerous work (B.$\bar{C}$.$\bar{D}$)

Without using the concepts of the hierarchical structure of the input data and chain-linked truth tables it would be difficult to compile a unique table to solve the problem. Such a table would look like the following: (E = Employee).

		E						
A	B	C	D	E				
0	0							
0	1	0	0	0				
0	1	0	0	1				
0	1	0	1	0				
0	1	0	1	1				
0	1	1	0	0				
0	1	1	0	1				
0	1	1	1	0				
0	1	1	1	1				
1	0							
1	1	0	0	0				
1	1	0	0	1				
1	1	0	1	0				
1	1	0	1	1				
1	1	1	0	0				
1	1	1	0	1				
1	1	1	1	0				
1	1	1	1	1				

In the two cases $\overline{B}.\overline{A}$ and $\overline{B}.A$, the codes C, D and E cannot be present and have no significance and thus cannot be noted in the table. On the other hand, by using the hierarchical structure of the input, three tables can be compiled:

- the first table for the set E and its sub-sets A and B (first level on the data diagram),
- the two other tables for the second level on the data diagram: one for the employee sub-set $B.\overline{A}$ and the other for the sub-set B.A (A table is required for every occurence of B since its structure is complex alternative).

The output structure is as follows: the problem statement indicates that the action for bonus V is executed for the set $\bar{B}$, and those for the others for the set B depending on the values C, D and E.

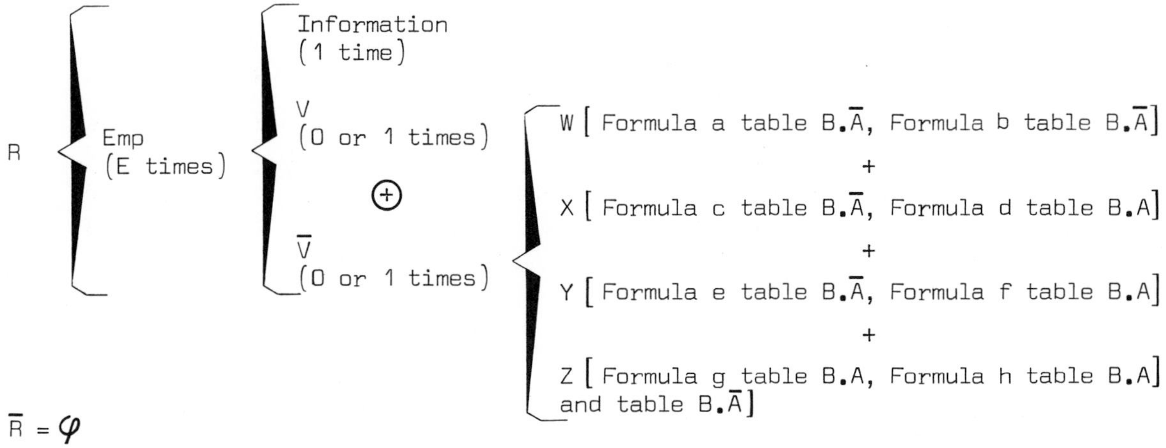

$\bar{R} = \varphi$

For a better understanding of the above diagram, remember that $\bar{A}$ indicates the temporary and A the permanent employees.

For result bonus Z note that:

- formula g is used in table B.A
- formula h is used in both table B.A and B.$\bar{A}$

since it is used for both temporary and permanent employees.

Here are the tables:

First level of input data:

| E | | V | Transfer to | Transfer to |
A B			B . $\bar{A}$	B . A
0 0		X		
0 1			X	
1 0		X		
1 1				X

Second level of input data: First table B.$\overline{A}$

B.$\overline{A}$ C D E	a	b	c	e	h
0 0 0	X				X
0 0 1	X			X	X
0 1 0	X		X		
0 1 1	X		X	X	
1 0 0		X			
1 0 1		X			
1 1 0		X			
1 1 1		X			

Second table B.A

B A C D E	d	f	g	h
0 0 0		X		X
0 0 1				X
0 1 0	X	X		
0 1 1	X			
1 0 0			X	
1 0 1			X	
1 1 0			X	
1 1 1			X	

The program is constructed and optimised by applying the rules already studied. At the level of table E, a tree structure is used. At the levels of tables B.$\overline{A}$ and B.A composite solutions are used.
The diagram of the program subdivision is:

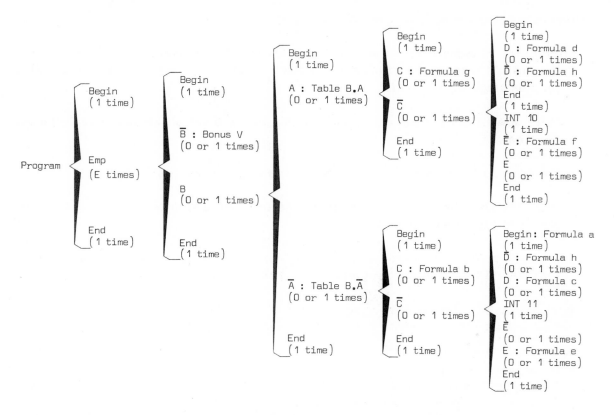

A program sub-set emanating from a table at a lower level is always included in a program sub-set emanating from the table at the next higher level.

THE RECONSTRUCTION OF A NON-HIERARCHICALLY ORGANISED PROGRAM

Today, and for many years yet, programs are the most often developed by the space-time approach and not by the hierarchical approach. The solutions obtained generally have a long processing time and above all are very difficult to understand which makes amendments very expensive. In the most favourable case, which is assumed for the example that follows, the reconstruction of an old program will not reduce processing speed nor core memory space. However, it will increase the clarity considerably.

When an old program, without a hierarchical structure, is to be amended, the ideal is to reconstruct it. If reconstruction takes longer, which is not necessarily the case, it has the immense advantage of preparing for easier future maintenance.

To reconstruct an old program, the following steps are required:

- **Draw the flowchart from the instruction listing. This flowchart must include all the branch instructions. Software of the 'AUTO-FLOW' type can be very useful for this stage of the work.**

- **Write down the Boolean expression for the data sub-set processed in each logical sequence.**

- **Compile truth tables from which the program can be reconstructed.**

- **Once the solution has been debugged, the program documentation is updated to facilitate future amendments.**

- **If amendments are required at the time when the program is being reconstructed, they should be noted in the tables to incorporate them in the new solution.**

Example: take a flowchart obtained from a sub-set of instructions from a listing. This program sub-set processes a data set E which includes 4 non-exclusive sub-sets A, B, C, D:

- A contains 1 element
- B contains 1 element
- C contains 1 element
- D contains n elements (n can be zero)

The procedures (sequences) are referred to by numbers from 1 through 8.

Here is the flowchart:

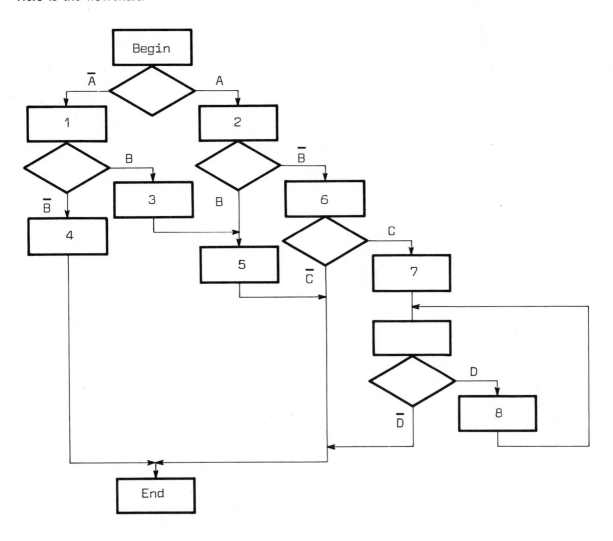

Note the sequence following sequence 7; it contains exactly one instruction, the branch which tests for the presence or absence of an element of the set D.

Here now is the list of the data sub-sets subject to the actions executed in the sequences:

1 = $\overline{A}$	5 = $\overline{A}.B + A.B = B$
2 = A	6 = $A.\overline{B}$
3 = $\overline{A}.B$	7 = $A.\overline{B}.C$
4 = $\overline{A}.\overline{B}$	8 = $A.\overline{B}.C.D$

From this list, the truth table can be compiled:

E A B C D	1	2	3	4	5	6	7	8
0 0 0 0	X			X				
0 0 0 1	X			X				
0 0 1 0	X			X				
0 0 1 1	X			X				
0 1 0 0	X		X		X			
0 1 0 1	X		X		X			
0 1 1 0	X		X		X			
0 1 1 1	X		X		X			
1 0 0 0		X				X		
1 0 0 1		X				X		
1 0 1 0		X				X	X	
1 0 1 1		X				X	X	X
1 1 0 0		X			X			
1 1 0 1		X			X			
1 1 1 0		X			X			
1 1 1 1		X			X			

The amendments required for this program sub-set are the following:

- action 9 = A. This action must be executed at the end of the processing of A.
- action 10 = A.$\bar{B}$.C.D. This action must be executed once for the group D at the end, but not at all if D contains no elements.

Here is the amended table:

E A B C D	1	2	3	4	5	6	7	8	9	10
0 0 0 0	X			X						
0 0 0 1	X			X						
0 0 1 0	X			X						
0 0 1 1	X			X						
0 1 0 0	X		X		X					
0 1 0 1	X		X		X					
0 1 1 0	X		X		X					
0 1 1 1	X		X		X					
1 0 0 0		X				X			X	
1 0 0 1		X				X			X	
1 0 1 0		X				X	X		X	
1 0 1 1		X				X	X	X	X	X
1 1 0 0		X			X				X	
1 1 0 1		X			X				X	
1 1 1 0		X			X				X	
1 1 1 1		X			X				X	

Diagram of the reconstructed and amended program:

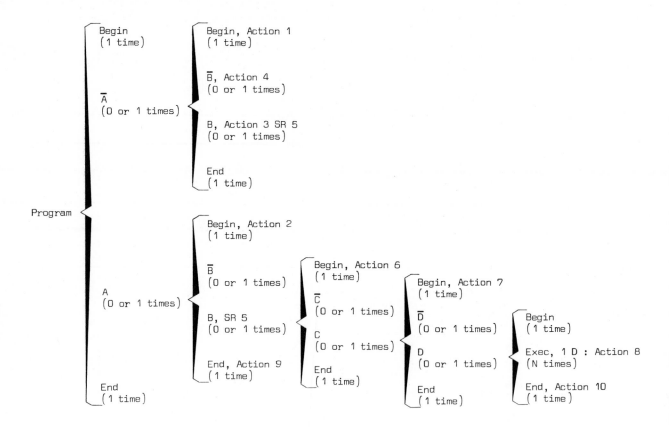

Here is the flowchart of the logical sequences of this amended program:

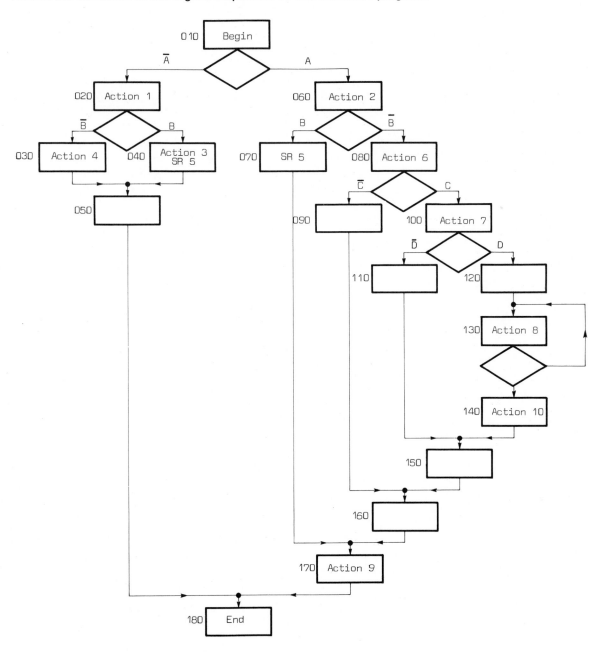

This solution only contains one more branch instruction than the original in spite of the amendments. Action 5 is managed by a sub-routine. This sub-routine is called twice: in sequences 040 and 070. The amendments caused no trouble:

- Action 9 is executed in sequence 070
- Action 10 is executed in sequence 140

Of course, the amendments could have been made on the old program, but not without a risk of error and not without adding more then one extra test.

The old solution has two defects:

- Action 5 was located in the intersection of 2 sets thus violating the rule: each sub-set must belong to exactly one set at the next higher level (mapping rule from chapter 2, part I). This defect can be illustrated by the VENN diagram:

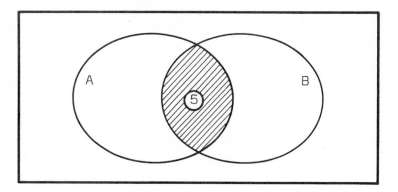

The consequence is that action 9 is difficult to program since it must be executed on the data set A but at the end.

The second defect is:

- The repetitive action 8 is not preceded by a begin and followed by an end. This makes it difficult to add action 10 which must be executed for the group of data sets D (when not empty) and at the end.

This gives an indication of the advantages of the hierarchical approach for program maintenance.

SUMMARY

- *When there are complex alternative structures at several consecutive levels in the data, for each one a truth table is compiled. Each table at a higher level transfers to at least one table at the next lower level.*

- *To reconstruct an old program developed by an empirical method the steps are:*

  — *draw a flowchart of the logical sequences,*
  — *write down the Boolean expression of the conditions for each sequence,*
  — *construct the program using the rules discussed in the preceding chapters,*
  — *revise the program documentation.*

EXERCISE

Updating a magazine subscribers' file.

Run diagram:

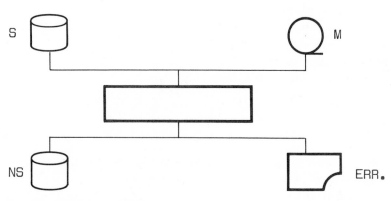

```
  S = Subscribers' file (before updating)
 NS = Subscribers' file (after updating)
  M = Movement file
ERR = Error file
```

RESULTS

New subscribers' file: 0 or 1 records per subscriber (0 if error):

Subs. Nº	Name Address	Conditions	Starting date	Finishing date

Error report file: 0 or 1 lines per subscriber (1 if error)

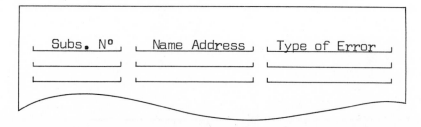

DATA

Subscribers' file: 0 or 1 records per subscriber:

Subs. Nº	Name Address	Conditions	Starting date	Finishing date

Constant: Date to-day

Movement file: 0 or 1 records per subscriber:

Subs. Nº	Name Address	Conditions	Starting date	Finishing date	Code X	Y

The code field can take the values:
$\overline{X}.\overline{Y}$ = Delete the subscriber record (DEL)
$\overline{X}.Y$ = Replace the subscriber record (REP)
$X.\overline{Y}$ = Create a subscriber record (CRE)
$X.Y$ = Error condition — impossible code (CODE)

PROCESSING

If $\overline{M}.S$ duplicate the old record unless the finishing date has been reached.
If there is a movement record (M):
- $M.\overline{S}$ and $X.\overline{Y}$: CREATION
- $M.S$ and $\overline{X}.Y$: REPLACE
- $M.S$ and $\overline{X}.\overline{Y}$: DELETE
- $M.S$ and finishing date reached: DELETE (Whatever the value of the code)

ERRORS

- $M.\overline{S}$ and $\overline{X}.Y$: REPLACE a non-existing subscriber
- $M.\overline{S}$ and $\overline{X}.\overline{Y}$: DELETE a non-existing subscriber
- $M.S$ and $X.\overline{Y}$: CREATE an existing subscriber
- $X.Y$: IMPOSSIBLE code

Do this problem completely and after having checked your solution by using the Results see the solution in the pages that follow:

SOLUTION

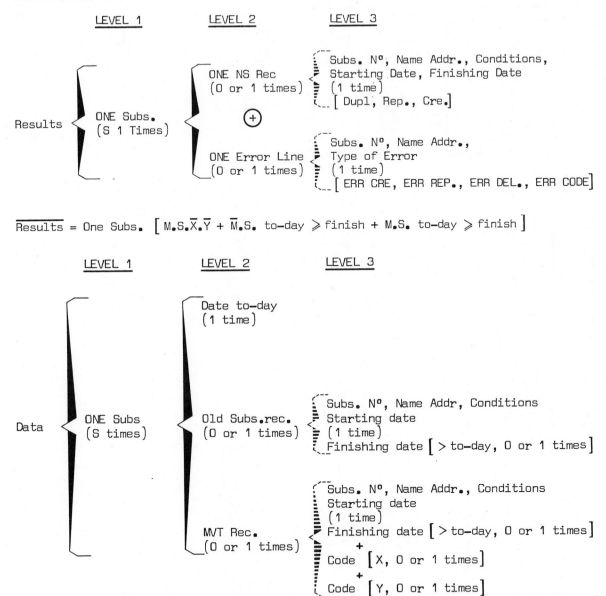

$$\overline{\text{Results}} = \text{One Subs.} \left[\text{M.S.}\overline{\text{X}}.\overline{\text{Y}} + \overline{\text{M}}.\text{S. to-day} \geqslant \text{finish} + \text{M.S. to-day} \geqslant \text{finish} \right]$$

Table T 10

1 SUBS.		DUPL or DEL	T 20	T 21
S	M			
0	0	φ	φ	φ
0	1		X	
1	0	X		
1	1			X

S = Subs. Rec
M = MVT Rec.
DUPL or DEL = Duplicate
Unless Finishing date reached.

Table T 20

1 SUBS.		CRE	ERR CODE	ERR REP	ERR DEL
$\bar{S}$ X	M Y				
0	0				X
0	1			X	
1	0	X			
1	1		X		

$\bar{X}.\bar{Y}$ = DEL .
$\bar{X}.Y$ = REP
$X.\bar{Y}$ = CRE
$X.Y$ = CODE (error)

Table T 21

1 SUBS S.M			REP	ERR CRE	ERR CODE	DEL
Exp.	X	Y				
0	0	0				X
0	0	1	X			
0	1	0		X		
0	1	1			X	
1	0	0				X
1	0	1				X
1	1	0				X
1	1	1				X

Exp. = Finishing data reached
The variable Exp. does not appear in table 20 since the case of Finishing date reached cannot occur for a new subscriber.

Program preparation from the tables:

- T 10: DUPL. (or DEL) = $\bar{M}$
  Transfer to T 20 = $M.\bar{S}$
  Transfer to T 21 = $M.S$

- T 20: ERR. DEL. $\quad = \bar{X}.\bar{Y}$
  ERR. REP. $\quad = \bar{X}.Y$
  CRE $\quad\quad\quad = X.\bar{Y}$
  ERR. CODE $\quad = X.Y$

- T 21: DEL 1 $\quad\quad = $ Exp.
  DEL 2 $\quad\quad = \overline{Exp}.\, \bar{X}.\bar{Y}$
  REP $\quad\quad\quad = \overline{Exp}.\, \bar{X}.Y$
  ERR. CRE $\quad = \overline{Exp}.\, X.\bar{Y}$
  ERR. CODE $= \overline{Exp}.\, X.Y$

Program diagram:

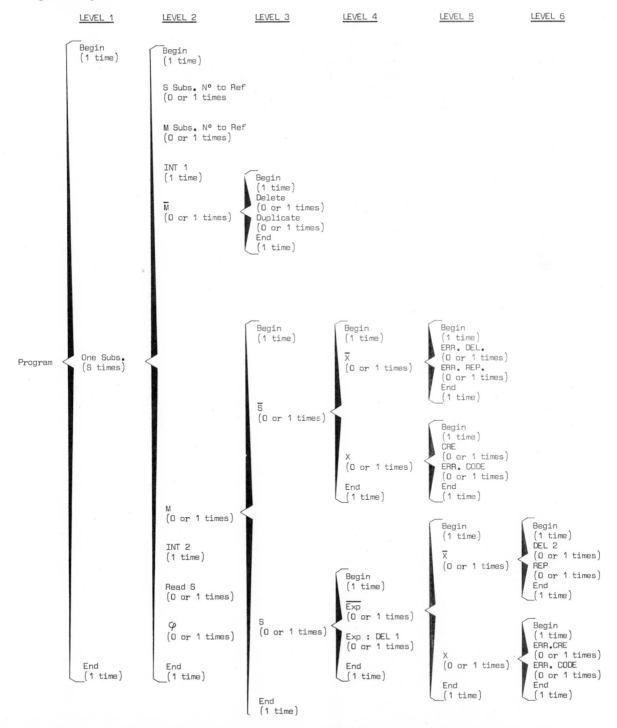

Flowchart up to level 3.

As in the exercise at the end of the preceding chapter, this flowchart will not be a sequence flow-chart but a flowchart of the first three hierarchical levels.

The sub-sets T 20 and T 21 are not logical sequences and their flowcharts are on the following page. When the flowchart is too big, in order to maintain an overall view of the program, it is preferable to break it up in hierarchical sections rather than in the usual space-time sections.

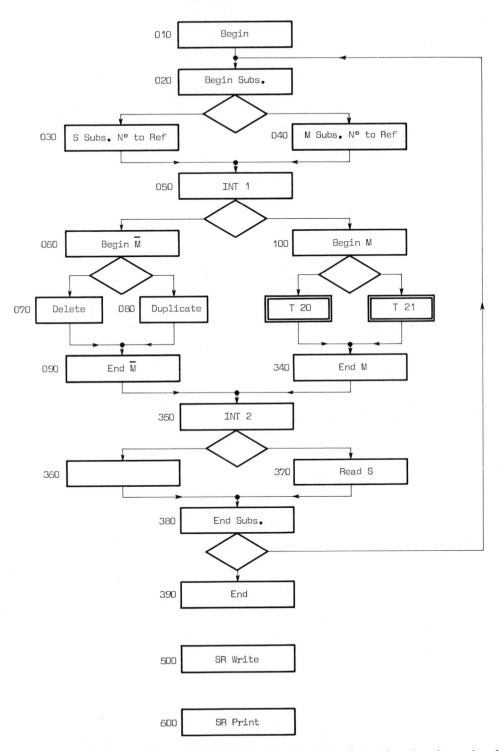

Note: the matching of the two files can be further simplified by eliminating the alternative 030 and 040 and by storing the appropriate reference criterion.

Sequence flowchart for the sub-set T 20:

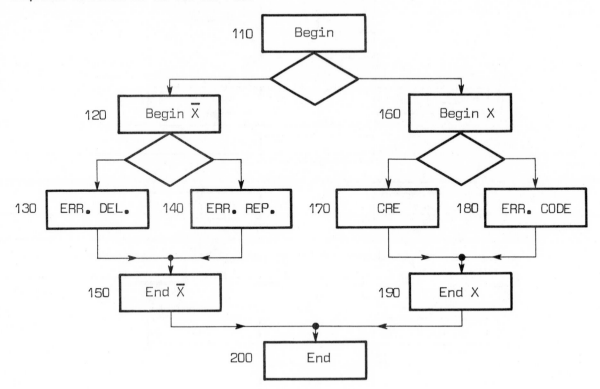

Sequence flowchart for the sub-set T 21:

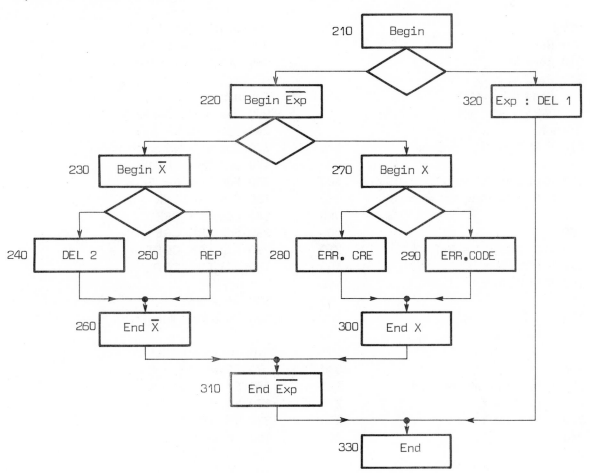

Detailed organisation : Instruction Lists by Type

Read

010 Read S
010 Read M
340 Read M
370 Read S

Branch

020 If M Subs N° < S Subs N°	040	
030	050	
050 If M Subs N° = Ref	100	
060 If S Finish date not reached	080	
070	090	
090	350	
100 If S Subs N° = Ref	210	
110 If M code X	160	
120 If M Code Y	140	
130	150	
150	200	
160 If M Code Y	180	
170	190	
200	340	
210 If M Finish date reached	320	
220 If M Code X	270	
230 If M Code Y	250	
240	260	
260	310	
270 If M code Y	290	
280	300	
310	330	
350 If S Subs N° = Ref	370	
360	380	
380 If $\overline{\text{EOF}}$ (both)	020	

Preparation of Branch

030 S Subs N° to Ref
040 M Subs N° to Ref

Output

070 Space to NS area
240 Space to NS area
320 Space to NS area
170 Edit Created Subs
250 Edit Replaced Subs
130 Edit ERR. DEL
140 Edit ERR. REP
280 Edit ERR. CRE
290 Edit ERR. CODE
180 Edit ERR. CODE

500 Write NS
600 Print Error line

Sub-routine Calls

070 SR WRITE
260 SR WRITE
170 SR WRITE
320 SR WRITE
150 SR PRINT
300 SR PRINT
180 SR PRINT

Because the subscribers' file is on disc storage, it is unnecessary to program any action for duplicating records. To delete records, however, action must be taken according to the software conventions; here it is assumed that the convention is to move spaces to the output record area (i.e. in sequences 070, 240 320).

Sorted List of Instructions

010	Read S	
	Read M	
020	If M Subs. N° < S Subs N°	040
030	S Subs. N° to Ref field	050
040	M Subs. N° to Ref Field	
050	If M Subs. N° = Ref	100
060	If S Finish date not reached	080
070	Space to NS area	
	Call SR WRITE	090
080		
090		350
100	If S Subs. N° = Ref	210
110	If M Code X	160
120	If M Code Y	140
130	Edit ERR. DEL	150
140	Edit ERR. REP	
150	Call SR PRINT	
160	If M code Y	180
170	Edit Created Rec	
	Call SR WRITE	190
180	Edit ERR. CODE	
	Call SR PRINT	
190		
200		340
210	If M Finish date reached	320
220	If M Code X	270
230	If M Code Y	250
240	Space to NS area	260
250	Edit Replaced record	
260	Call SR WRITE	310
270	If M Code Y	290
280	Edit ERR. CRE	300
290	Edit ERR. CODE	
300	Call SR PRINT	
310		330

320	Space to NS area	
	Call SR WRITE	
330		
340	Read M	
350	If S Subs N° = Ref	370
360		380
370	Read S	
380	If $\overline{\text{EOF-M}} + \overline{\text{EOF-S}}$	020

SR WRITE

500 WRITE NS

SR PRINT

600 Print Error line and Restore

4 — THE PROCESSING PHASES

DEFINITION OF THE PHASES

Conditional branch instructions determine completely the logic of a program. Their execution depends on the result of a comparison between an identification criterion which accompanies data and a reference criterion which is saved in core memory. This is why the logic of a program can be deduced from the input data structure. This is only possible as long as the input data sub-sets are accompanied by their identification criteria: a value or an identifier.

When the processing required by the problem statement is performed on sub-sets whose elements are not identifiable at input, the necessary identification criteria must be created during the running of the program: switches, counters or intermediate results of calculations.

When a branch instruction uses an identification criterion created by program, there is a change of processing phase.

DEFINITION

Every program includes at least 1 processing phase. The processing phases, other than the first, are program sub-sets which process data sub-sets whose identification criteria, not present at input, have been created by instructions belonging to the preceding phases of the program.

The data, subject to processing, may or may not have been generated during the program.

The creation of missing *reference criteria* during the program does not mean there is a change of phase. Only missing *identification criteria* involve a change of phase.

The hierarchical diagram of the input data allows the first phase to be constructed.

RULE

When a program includes two or more phases, data diagrams must be drawn for the data input to the second phase and those following. These diagrams are constructed by applying the same rules as used for the input data.

RULE

The structure of the program sub-set corresponding to a processing phase is deduced from that of the data input to that phase by applying the same rules as those concerning the data input to the program.

RULE

The data set input to a phase, other than to the first, is a sub-set of the results set of the preceding phase. Because of this, the latter set must be considered in order to determine the actions noted in the truth tables and to validate the program. Thus actions which generate data input to phases must be noted as in an output data diagram.

Programs with several phases are frequently found in business informatics and even more in scientific informatics.

An identification criterion is most often determined during the running of a program by:

— a switch setting
— an operation for counting
— a calculation

EXAMPLES

SWITCH SETTING: A stock file is to be processed by product. An error record or a new stock record is to be obtained for each product. Suppose that there are several possible error conditions and several ways of calculating the new stock.

Starting from the input data, all the cases can be processed but there is no initial identification criterion indicating whether a product does or does not belong to the sub-set of products for which there is an error. To do this, a switch can be used whose value at the end of the product processing sub-set allows a product to be identified (error or new stock) and thus ensuring that the outputs are correctly programmed.

COUNTING: a listing with 30 lines per page is to be produced. After the 30th line, the paper must be advanced to the top of the next page on the printer.

The problem here is to identify the 30th line of each page. At the start of a page a counter is cleared. At each line, 1 is added to the counter, and the counter's contents (identification criterion) are compared with a constant 30 (reference criterion) to determine whether or not the line belongs to the set of the lines that are followed by a paper slew to top of page. If the printing of the lines belongs to phase 1, the page change belongs to phase 2. It cannot be deduced from the input data diagram. The diagram of data input to phase 2 is:

$$\text{UNIVERSAL SET} \quad \left\{ \begin{array}{l} \text{COUNTER} \geqslant 30 \\ (0 \text{ or } 1 \text{ times}) \end{array} \right.$$
$$\text{1 LINE}$$

By applying the rule: 'if the data structure is alternative, so is the corresponding program structure', the following program sub-set is obtained:

$$
\text{Process One Line} \left\{
\begin{array}{l}
\text{Begin} \\
(\,1 \text{ time}\,) \\[1ex]
\text{Change Page} \\
(\,0 \text{ or } 1 \text{ times}\,) \\[1ex]
\varphi \\
(\,0 \text{ or } 1 \text{ times}\,) \\[1ex]
\text{End} \\
(\,1 \text{ time}\,)
\end{array}
\right.
$$

CALCULATION: the durations of jobs are to be calculated from job cards:

$$
\text{Input Job Card} \atop (\,J \text{ times}\,) \left\{
\begin{array}{l}
\text{Job N}^{\text{o}} \\
(\,1 \text{ time}\,) \\[1ex]
\text{Starting Time} \\
(\,1 \text{ time}\,) \\[1ex]
\text{Finishing Time} \\
(\,1 \text{ time}\,)
\end{array}
\right.
$$

The times on the card are punched automatically by a device electronically controlled by a clock. The plant normally operates on a 24 hour-day basis. The duration is calculated by the difference between starting and finishing times i.e. difference = finishing time — starting time. When the starting time is greater than the finishing time the difference will be negative and the duration will be (24 + difference).

The input data do not determine which formula is to be used (i.e. difference if non-negative or 24 + difference if negative). The data input to phase 2 after calculating the difference will be:

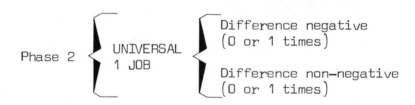

The program is constructed first of all by using the input:

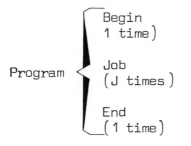

The program is terminated by using the data input to phase 2:

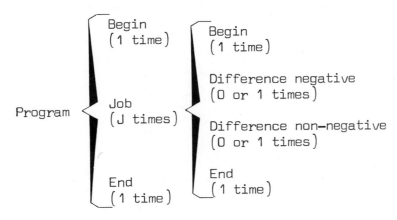

Here is the flowchart:

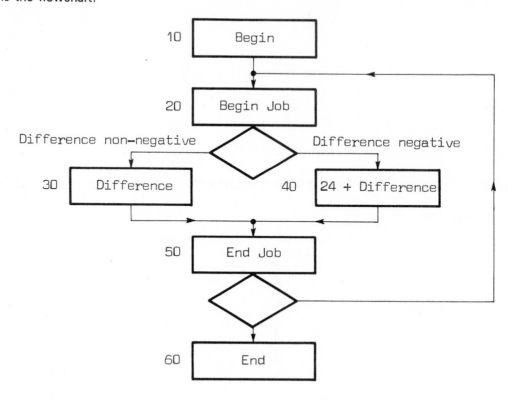

Phase 2 includes the last instruction of sequence 20 and the sequences 30 and 40; the other sequences and instructions belong to phase 1.

A program sub-set emanating from a phase other than the first is always included in the set emanating from the input data (phase 1).

Thus it can be seen that processing phases take place in hierarchical order and not in space-time order. The hierarchical approach allows the phase organisation to be clearly perceived.

GENERAL RECAPITULATION

Throughout the following example, the principal rules outlined in this book will be reviewed. It will be followed by a summary of the steps that a program designer should go through to accomplish his task successfully.

Example: A stock updating problem with automatic restock orders when stock becomes low.

Run diagram:

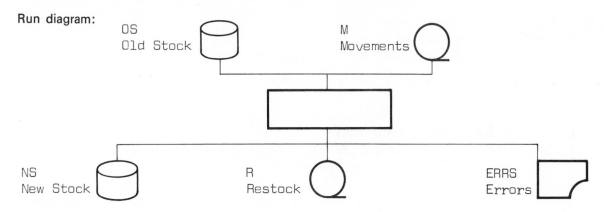

Input data:

— File OS, Old Stock (0 or 1 records per product)

| Prod N° | Quantity | Max. Stock | Mini Stock |

— File M, Movements (0 or M records per product)

| Prod N° | Quantity |

- • The Old Stock quantity has already been verified by a previous program and cannot be less than the Minimum Stock.

— Texts indicating errors:

- • a text indicating New Stock quantity negative (NS<O)
- • a text indicating that there was no Old Stock record ($\overline{OS}$)

Output results:

— file NS, New Stock (0 or 1 records per product)

| Prod N° | Quantity | Max. Stock | Mini Stock |

— file R, Restock orders (0 or 1 records per product)

| Prod N° | Quantity |

— Error report (0 or 1 lines per product)

| Prod N° | Text indicating Error |

There is an error, for a given product, when:
— the Old Stock record is missing
— the New Stock quantity is negative after the calculations.

When there is an error, no New Stock record is written.

Processing:

— if OS.$\overline{M}$, then NS quantity = OS quantity
— if OS.M, then NS quantity = OS quantity ± M quantity (algebraic sum)
— if (NS quantity < Min. Stock) and (NS quantity non-negative), then Restock Quantity = Max. Stock — NS Quantity
— if (NS Quantity < Min. Stock) and (NS Quantity negative) then NS Quantity is cleared giving: Restock Quantity = Max. Stock

Here is the output diagram:

$\overline{\text{Results}} = \varphi$

The sign + is used at level 2, although strictly speaking a New Stock and an error record are mutually exclusive, but each is compatible with a Restock record.

Here is the diagram of the input data:

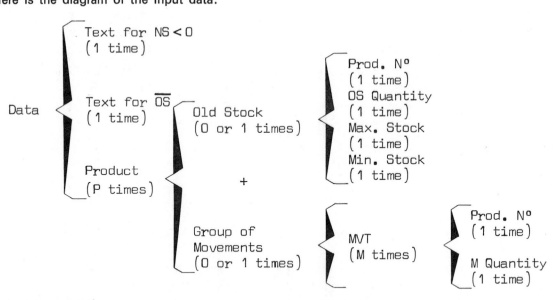

Processing phase:
the New Stock quantity constitutes an identification criterion determining whether or not the data concerning a product belong to the following data sub-sets:
— the data set concerning products for which there is an error condition,
— the data set concerning products for which restock orders are required,
— the data set concerning products for which a New-Stock record is created.

Here is the diagram of the data input to Phase 2 (sub-set of the results output from Phase 1):

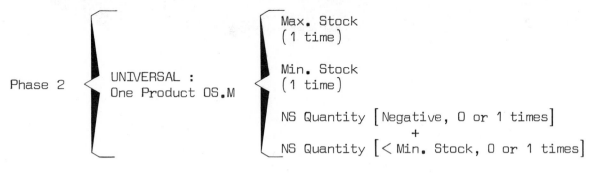

The program is constructed in stages. First of all, here is the truth table compiled from the input data and results:

| 1 Product | | ERR. | DUPL. | CALC. |
OS	M	$\overline{OS}$	OS	NS
0	0	φ	φ	φ
0	1	X		
1	0		X	
1	1			X

Note that the action CALC NS will produce a result output from phase 1 and input to phase 2.

The program levels corresponding to phase 1 are now constructed. At the first level, the rule used is: 'if the data structure is repetitive, so is the corresponding program structure'.
At levels 2 and 3, the table is used and once again the rule is applied in order to process the movements. This is a case when N can be zero. Finally, the reference criterion of each product must be determined and the Read instructions must be organised (multiple sources of input).

Here is the diagram for phase 1 of the program:

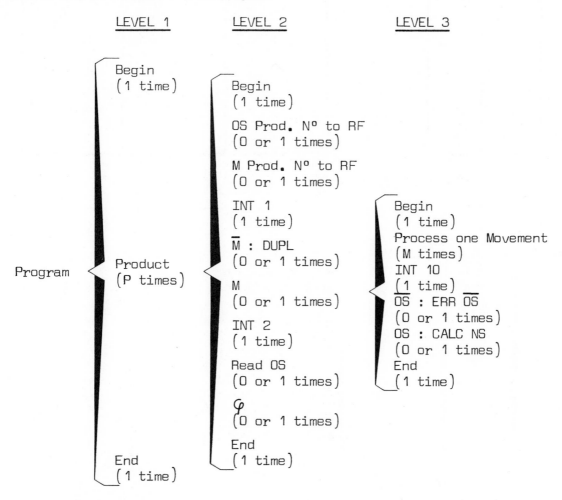

LEVEL 1   LEVEL 2   LEVEL 3

Program — Product (P times):
- Begin (1 time)
- Product (P times)
- End (1 time)

Level 2 (Product, P times):
- Begin (1 time)
- OS Prod. N° to RF (0 or 1 times)
- M Prod. N° to RF (0 or 1 times)
- INT 1 (1 time)
- $\overline{M}$: DUPL (0 or 1 times)
- M (0 or 1 times)
- INT 2 (1 time)
- Read OS (0 or 1 times)
- φ (0 or 1 times)
- End (1 time)

Level 3:
- Begin (1 time)
- Process one Movement (M times)
- INT 10 (1 time)
- $\overline{OS}$: ERR $\overline{OS}$ (0 or 1 times)
- OS : CALC NS (0 or 1 times)
- End (1 time)

Note the structures used at the different levels:

— simple repetitive at Level 1,
— complex alternative at Level 2,
— complex mixed at Level 3.

Now construct the table emanating from the data input to phase 2.
Let X be the sub-set of products for which NS quantity < 0.
Let Y be the sub-set of products for which NS quantity < Min. Stock.

| 1 Product OS. M | | Output NS | Err NS < 0 | Clear NS Quantity | Output Restock |
X	Y				
0	0	X			
0	1	X			X
1	0	φ	φ	φ	φ
1	1		X	X	X

Here now is the complete program diagram:

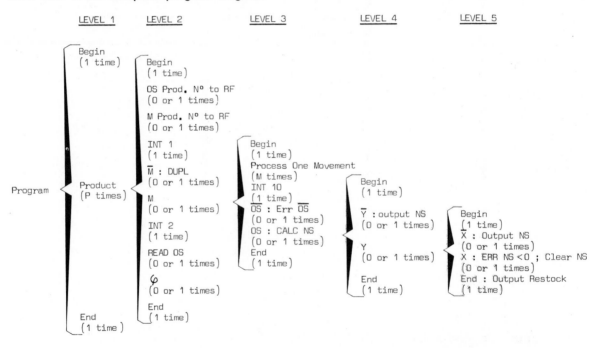

Note at levels 4 and 5 the tree structure: a composite solution could have been used but the tree is preferable since it is favorable to the most frequently occurring case; i.e. New Stock quantity neither negative nor less than Min. Stock.

The composite solution would have been:

LEVEL 4

```
Begin
(1 time)

X̄ : Output NS
(0 or 1 times)

X : ERR NS  0 ; Clear NS
(0 or 1 times)

INT 20
(1 time)

Ȳ
(0 or 1 times)

Y : Output Restock
(0 or 1 times)

End
(1 time)
```

Note that this *is* a composite solution and not a complex alternative since actions occur in both branches of the first simple alternative (i.e. in cases X̄ and X) whereas in a complex alternative, one branch of each simple alternative is always empty.

Flowchart of the logical sequences:

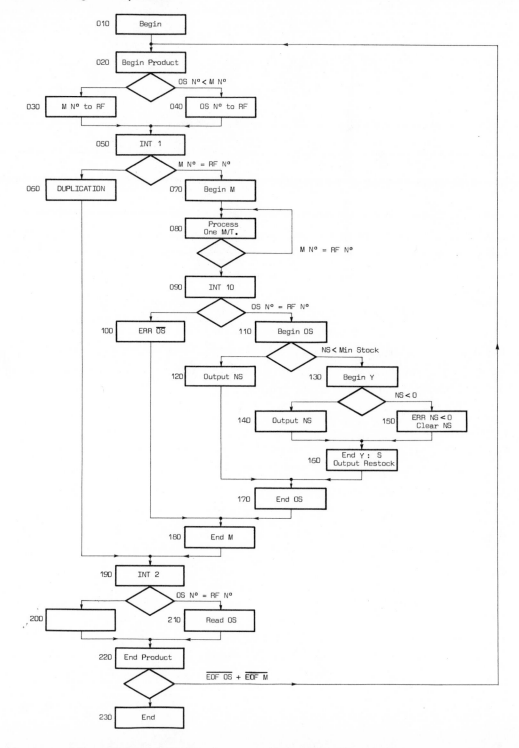

Processing phase 2 includes sequences 120 through 160 and the last instruction of sequence 110.

Detailed organisation:

— Reads   :   010 — 1st READ OS
                  010 — 1st READ M
                  080 — READ OS
                  210 — READ M

— Branches :   020 — If OS N°<M N°   040
                  030 —   050
                  050 — If M N° = RF N°   070
                  060 —   190
                  080 — If M N° = RF N°   080
                  090 — If OS N° = RF N°   110
                  100 —   180
                  110 — If NS Qty<Min. Stock   130
                  120 —   170
                  130 — If NS Qty<0   150
                  140 —   160
                  190 — If OS N° = RF N°   210
                  200 —   220
                  220 — If $\overline{\text{EOF OS}}$ + $\overline{\text{EOF M}}$ 020

— Preparation of branches:

                  040 — OS N° to RF
                  030 — M N° to RF

Missing reference criteria are determined and stored in core memory by preparation of branch instructions. Missing identification criteria, such as the value of NS quantity, to be input to phase 2, are obtained by calculations. These calculations are noted in the next list:

— preparation of calculations and calculations:

    070 — Clear NS Quantity field
    080 — Add M Quantity to NS quantity
    110 — Add OS Quantity to NS Quantity
    150 — Clear NS Quantity field
    160 — Restock Quantity = Max. Stock — NS Quantity

— preparation of outputs and outputs:

100 — Edit ERR $\overline{\text{OS}}$	060 — Edit NS record	060 — Output NS Record
100 — Print and Restore	120 — Edit NS Record	120 — Output NS Record
150 — Edit ERR NS<0	140 — Edit NS Record	140 — Output NS Record
150 — Print and Restore		160 — Edit Restock Record
		160 — Output Restock Record

The results diagram can be used to verify this solution thus avoiding errors due to inattention such as forgetting one of the instructions for outputting the New Stock record. It should be noted that the editing and writing of the NS record can be managed by a sub-routine.

Finally here is the sorted list of instructions for this program:

010	1st READ OS	
	1st READ M	
020	IF OS N° < M N°	040
030	M N° to RF	050
040	OS N° to RF	
050	IF M N° = RF N°	070
060	Edit New Stock rec.	
	Write New Stock rec.	
070	Clear NS Quantity	
080	Add M Quantity to NS Quantity	
	READ M	
	IF M N° = RF N°	080
090	IF OS N° = RF N°	110
100	Edit ERR $\overline{OS}$	
	Print and Restore	180
110	Add OS Quantity to NS Quantity	
	IF NS Qty < Min. Stock	130
120	Edit NS rec.	
	Write NS rec.	170
130	IF NS Qty < 0	150
140	Edit NS Rec.	
	Write NS Rec.	160
150	Edit ERR NS < 0	
	Print and Restore	
	Clear NS Quantity	
160	Restock Quantity = Max. Stock — NS Qty	
	Edit Restock Record	
	Write Restock Record	
170		180
180		190
190	IF OS N° = RF N°	210
200		220
210	READ OS	
220	IF $\overline{EOF\ OS}$ + $\overline{EOF\ M}$	020
230		END

Note that the housekeeping types of instruction concerning the computer and peripherals such as the opening and closing of files, are not noted in the list. The programmer must make provisions to include them when he codes the program in the appropriate language.

The example just given is a fairly complete overview of the approach used by an informatician to construct a program.

To finish, here is a general summary of the steps used to construct a program:

PREPARATION

- 1 — Draw the results diagram
- 2 — Draw the input diagram
- 3 — Draw the diagram for the absence of output (results)
- 4 — Draw, if necessary, the phase diagram (s)
- 5 — Note actions that produce output and data to be input to the phases
- 6 — Compile truth tables as required

TO OBTAIN THE ORGANISATION OF THE LOGICAL SEQUENCES

- 7 — Construct the program level by level, starting from the highest, by using the input diagram, the phase diagrams and the tables
- 8 — Draw the sequence flowchart and number the sequences
- 9 — Verify the flowchart by using the results, the phase and the results diagrams

DETAILED ORGANISATION

- 10 — Draw up lists of instructions by type: Reads, branches, preparation of branches, preparation of calculations and calculations, preparations of outputs and outputs, subroutine calls
- 11 — Draw up the sorted instruction list of the program
- 12 — Verify the program once more by using the results, the phases and the results diagrams

EXERCISE

In an enterprise, each employee's contribution to a mutual pension fund is calculated by 2 different formulae according to whether his salary does or does not exceed a limit fixed by the trustees of the fund.

Every month, each employee's contribution is calculated by using a monthly limit. Since salaries fluctuate, each employee's monthly contributions are not uniform and an adjustment is made every 6 months using a 6 monthly limit.

A program to calculate this adjustment is required.

RESULTS

Report:

0 or 1 lines per employee; 1 for each employee for whom an adjustment is required.

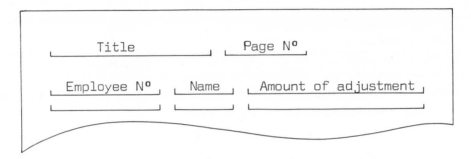

DATA

Constant:

> | 6 Monthly Limit |

File:

| Employee Nº | Name | Salary | Contribution |

There is one record for each month worked and paid for per employee.

PROCESSING

Accumulate the salaries and contributions for each employee. If total salaries > 6 monthly limit calculate the half-yearly contribution by formula 1 otherwise use formula 2.

Calculate the amount of adjustment: = half-yearly contribution — Total contributions.

If the adjustment is positive print a line for this employee otherwise do not output anything for this employee.

Do this problem completely and then compare your solution with that outlined on the following pages.

SOLUTION

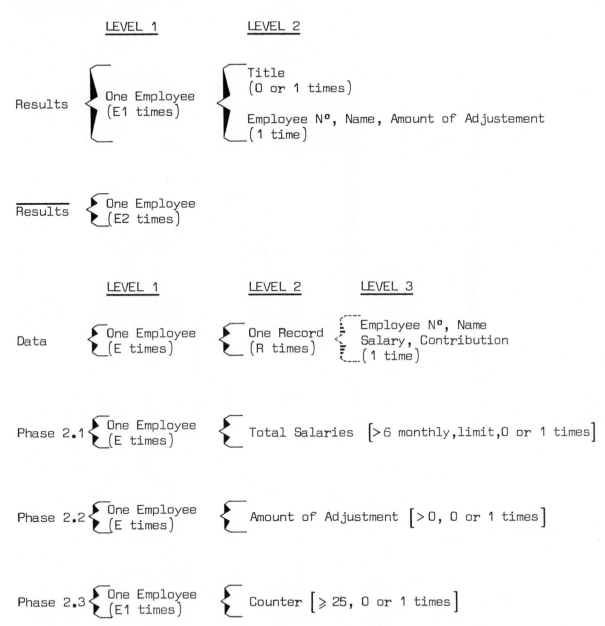

LEVEL 1   LEVEL 2

Results { One Employee (E1 times) }   { Title (O or 1 times)

Employee Nº, Name, Amount of Adjustement (1 time) }

Results { One Employee (E2 times) }

LEVEL 1   LEVEL 2   LEVEL 3

Data { One Employee (E times) }   { One Record (R times) }   { Employee Nº, Name Salary, Contribution (1 time) }

Phase 2.1 { One Employee (E times) }   { Total Salaries [>6 monthly,limit,O or 1 times] }

Phase 2.2 { One Employee (E times) }   { Amount of Adjustment [>0, O or 1 times] }

Phase 2.3 { One Employee (E1 times) }   { Counter [⩾ 25, O or 1 times] }

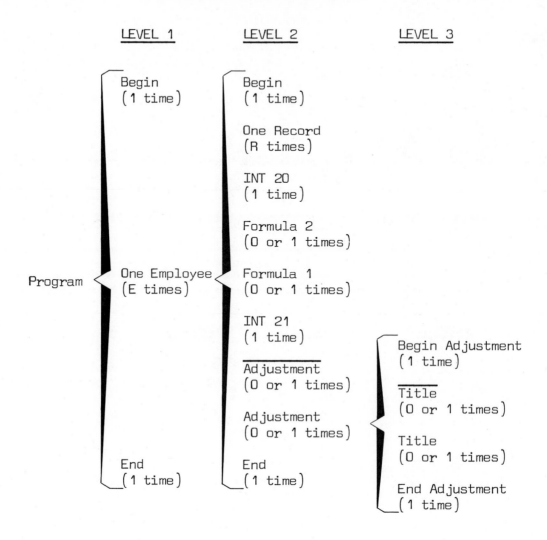

LEVEL 1   LEVEL 2   LEVEL 3

Program ⟨ One Employee (E times) ⟨

Begin
(1 time)

One Employee
(E times)

End
(1 time)

Begin
(1 time)

One Record
(R times)

INT 20
(1 time)

Formula 2
(0 or 1 times)

Formula 1
(0 or 1 times)

INT 21
(1 time)

Adjustment
(0 or 1 times)

Adjustment
(0 or 1 times)

End
(1 time)

Begin Adjustment
(1 time)

Title
(0 or 1 times)

Title
(0 or 1 times)

End Adjustment
(1 time)

Flowchart:

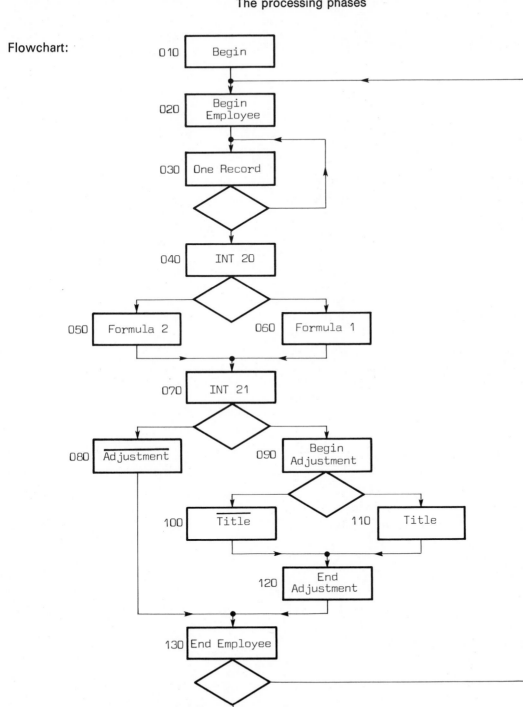

Detailed organisation: Instruction Lists by Type

Read
010 Read
030 Read

Branch

030 If Emp. N° = Ref N°	030
040 If Tot. Salary>6 monthly limit	060
050	070
070 If Adjustment>0	090
080	130
090 If counter ⩾25	110
100	120
130 If $\overline{\text{EOF}}$	020

Preparation of Branch
020 Transfer Emp. N° to Ref N°
010 Set Counter to 25
120 Add 1 to Counter
110 Clear Counter

Calculations
010 Clear page N°
030 Add Salary to Tot. Salary
030 Add Contrib. to Tot. Contrib.
050 Calculate $\frac{1}{2}$ yearly contrib. by Formula 2
060 Calculate $\frac{1}{2}$ yearly contrib. by Formula 1
070 Calc. Adjust. = $\frac{1}{2}$ yearly contrib. — Tot. contrib.
110 Add 1 to page N°
020 Clear Tot. Salary
020 Clear Tot. Contrib.

Output
020 Transfer Emp. Name to Ref Name
110 Edit Title and Page N°
110 Print Title and Restore
120 Edit Ref N° and Ref. Name
120 Edit Adjustment
120 Print and Restore

Detailed organisation: Sorted Instruction List in Sequence Order

```
010 Read
    Set Counter to 25
    Clear Page N°
020 Transfer Emp. N° to Ref N°
    Transfer Emp. Name to Ref. Name
    Clear Tot. Salary
    Clear Tot. Contrib.
030 Add Salary to Tot. Salary
    Add Contr. to Tot Contrib.
    Read
    If Emp. N° = Ref. N°                030
040 If Tot. Salary > 6 monthly limit   060
050 Calculate ½ yr. Cont. Formula 2    070
060 Calculate ½ yr. Cont. Formula 1
070 Calculate :
    Adjust. = ½ yr. cont. — Tot. Contrib.
    If Adjust. > 0                      090
080                                     130
090 If Counter ⩾ 25                     110
100                                     120
110 Clear Counter
    Add 1 to page N°
    Edit Title and page N°
    Print Title and Restore
120 Edit Ref N° and Ref. Name
    Edit Adjustment
    Print and Restore
    Add 1 to Counter
130 IF EOF                              020
140 Stop
```

EXERCISE

It is required to produce a report of invoices sent out to customers during the past year showing their total amount per customer.

Depending on the size of the total, a discount may be allowed.

RESULTS

Report:

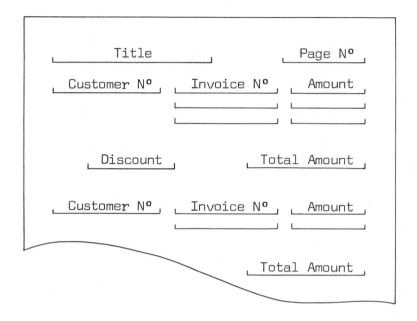

Start a new page every 30 lines, unless the 30th line is a total, in which case output the total line before starting a new page.

DATA

File:
One record per document, several documents per customer. File sorted on customer N°. If the code is I, the document is an Invoice otherwise it is a credit.

Customer N°	Invoice N°	Amount	Code

PROCESSING

If the file is empty or contains only credits, no output should be produced. If a customer only has credits, nothing should be output for that customer since credits must not be taken into account.

Accumulate the amounts of the invoices (if any) for each customer (if any). If this total is less than

10,000 dollars no discount is allowed. If it is between 10,000 and 49,999 dollars a discount of 1% is allowed. If it is between 50,000 and 99,999 dollars a discount of 2% is allowed. If it is greater than or equal to 100,000 dollars a discount of 5% is allowed.

Do this problem completely and then compare your solution with that proposed in the following pages (do not be surprised if your solution differs from that given since there are several different approaches to this problem).

SOLUTION

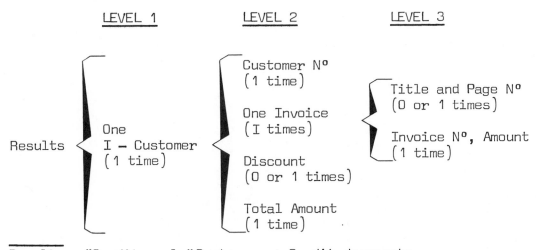

Results = "Credits only" Customers + Credit documents

I-Customer = Customer having at least 1 invoice.

In this solution, the data file has been subdivided into sub-sets which are strings of sub-sets — records, customers and documents:

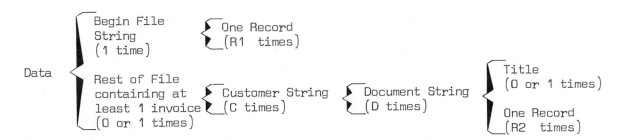

'Begin File String' is a string of records (1 or many) where the last one is EOF or an Invoice.
'Customer String' is a string of customer sub-sets (1 or many) where the first one is an I-Customer and the others are 'Credits only' customers.
'Document String' is a string of document records (1 or many) where the last one is an Invoice.

$$
\text{Phase 2}
\begin{cases}
\text{One} \\
\text{I} - \text{Customer}
\end{cases}
\begin{cases}
\text{Total Amount } \left[> 10{,}000,\ 0 \text{ or } 1 \text{ times} \right] \\
\qquad + \qquad\qquad + \\
\text{Total Amount } \left[\geqslant 50{,}000,\ 0 \text{ or } 1 \text{ times} \right] \\
\qquad + \qquad\qquad + \\
\text{Total Amount } \left[> 100{,}000,\ 0 \text{ or } 1 \text{ times} \right]
\end{cases}
$$

To deal with the credit document records, a READ sub-routine is set up:

$$
\text{SR READ}
\begin{cases}
\text{Begin} \\
(1 \text{ time}) \\
\\
\text{Read} \\
(\text{N times}) \\
\\
\text{End} \\
(1 \text{ time})
\end{cases}
$$

If a record is a credit document, another record is read. Thus after using the sub-routine it is certain that the record currently available is either EOF or an Invoice.

Truth table for Phase 2:

| One I – Customer | | | Discount | 1 % Discount | 2 % Discount | 5 % Discount |
10 K	50 K	100 K	Discount	Discount	Discount	Discount
0	0	0	Ẋ			
0	0	1	φ	φ	φ	φ
0	1	0	φ	φ	φ	φ
0	1	1	φ	φ	φ	φ
1	0	0		X		
1	0	1	φ	φ	φ	φ
1	1	0			X	
1	1	1				X

Where   10 K means Tot. Amount ⩾   10,000
         50 K means Tot. Amount ⩾   50,000
        100 K means Tot. Amount ⩾ 100,000

$\overline{\text{Discount}}$ = $\overline{\text{10 K}}$
1% Discount = 10 K. $\overline{\text{50 K.}}$
2% Discount =   50 K. $\overline{\text{100 K.}}$
5% Discount =   100 K.

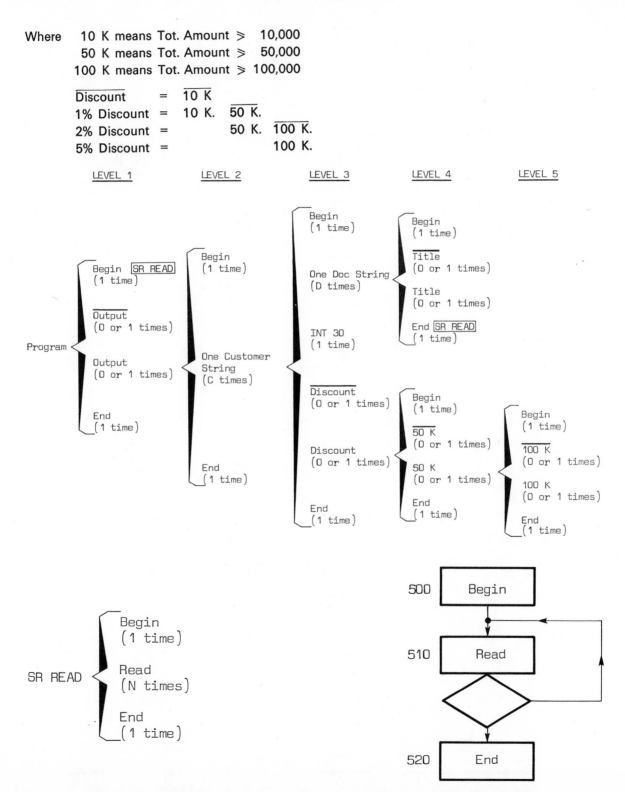

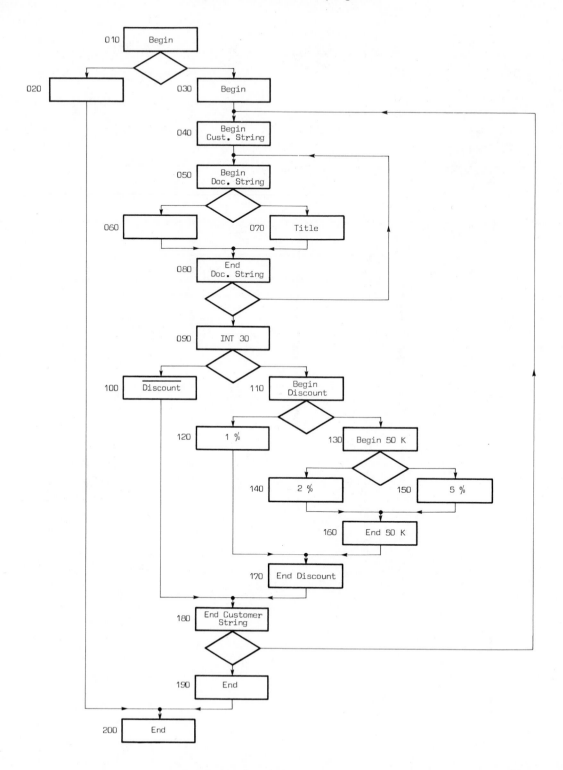

Read
510 Read

Branch
010 If $\overline{EOF}$		030
020		200
050 If Counter $\geqslant$ 30		070
060		080
080 If Cust. N° = Ref		050
090 If Tot. Amount $\geqslant$ 10 K		110
100		180
110 If Tot. Amount $\geqslant$ 50 K		130
120		170
130 If Tot. Amount $\geqslant$ 100 K		150
140		160
180 If $\overline{EOF}$		040
510 If Code $\neq$ I and $\overline{EOF}$		510

Preparation of Branch
030 Set Counter to 30
070 Clear Counter
080 Add 1 to Counter
040 Transfer Cust. N° to Ref

Calculations
070 Add 1 to page N°
080 Add Amount to Tot. Amount
120 Calc. Disc. 1%
140 Calc. Disc. 2%
150 Calc. Disc. 5%
040 Clear Tot. Amount

Output
080 Edit Ref. (Cust. N°)
080 Edit Invoice N° and Amount
080 Print and Restore
090 Edit Tot. Amount
170 Edit Discount
180 Print Total Line and Restore
070 Edit Title and Page N°
070 Print Title line and Restore

Sub-routine Calls
010 Call SR READ
080 Call SR READ

Detailed organisation: Sorted Instruction List

010 Call SR READ		SR READ	
If $\overline{\text{EOF}}$	030	500	
020	200	510 Read	
030 Set Counter to 30		If Code $\neq$ I	
040 Transfer Cust. N° to Ref		and $\overline{\text{EOF}}$	510
Clear Total Amount		520	
050 If Counter $\geqslant$ 30	070		
060	080		
070 Clear Counter			
Add 1 to page N°			
Edit Title and Page N°			
Print Title and Restore			
080 Add 1 to Counter			
Add Amount to Total Amount			
Edit Ref (Cust. N°)			
Edit Invoice N° and Amount			
Print and Restore			
Call SR READ			
If Cust. N° = Ref	050		
090 Edit Tot. Amount			
If Tot. Amount $\geqslant$ 10 K	110		
100	180		
110 If Tot. Amount $\geqslant$ 50 K	130		
120 Calc. Disc 1%	170		
130 If Tot. Amount $\geqslant$ 100 K	150		
140 Calc. Disc. 2%	160		
150 Calc. Disc. 5%			
160			
170 Edit Discount			
180 Print Total line and Restore			
If $\overline{\text{EOF}}$	040		
190			
200 Stop			

Note that other solutions are possible.

For example, the Data could have been subdivided (neglecting the discount) as follows:

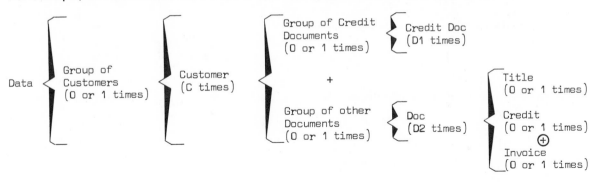

Which would have given:

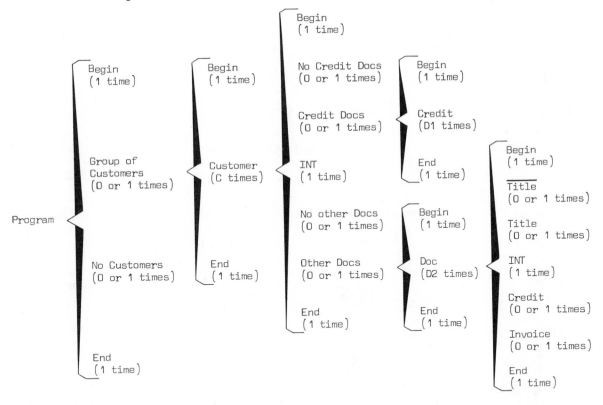

EXERCISE

In this problem the important thing is to determine clearly the processing phases. It concerns stock updating with automatic re-ordering.

DATA

Stock inputs file (0 or many records per product).

Product Nº.	Quantity	Value

Stock outputs file (0 or many records per product).

Product Nº	Quantity

Old stock file (0 or 1 records per product).

Product Nº	Quantity	Price	Value	Max.	Min.

Deletion file (0 or 1 records per product).

Product Nº

RESULTS

New Stock file (0 or 1 records per product): 0 if deleted or error.

Product Nº	Quantity	Price	Value	Max.	Min.

Re-order file (0 or 1 records per product); 1 if NS quantity< Min. and if the product is not deleted.

Product Nº	Quantity

Price difference file (0 or 1 records per product); 1 if the absolute difference between the Old Stock price and the New Stock price exceeds 10% of the Old Price and if the product is not deleted.

Product Nº	Old Price	New Price	Max.	Min.	Max. Value	Min. Value

Error report (0 or 1 records per product).

The errors are:
- no Old Stock record
- New Stock quantity negative when there is an Old Stock record
- Old Stock quantity less than Min. when there is neither Stock Input nor Output nor Deletion.
- Deletion of a product for which there is, in addition to an Old Stock record, a Stock Input.

RUN DIAGRAM

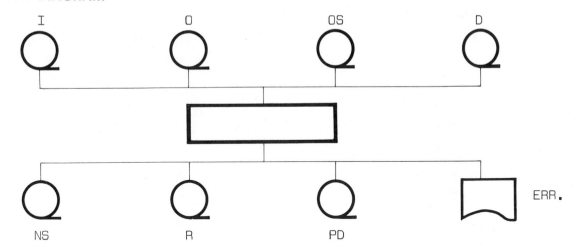

Processing:

For each product:

- If there is Stock Input, accumulate the quantities Input and the values Input. (Tot. Inp. Qty and Tot. Inp. value.)

- If there is Stock Output, accumulate the quantities Output. (Tot. Out. Qty.)

- If there is an Old Stock record without any movements, the N.S. quantity, price and value are set equal to those of the old stock record.

- If there is no Old Stock record, print an error line ERR $\overline{OS}$.

- If, with an Old Stock record there is Input, add the Old Stock and the Total Input quantities and values giving an intermediate quantity IQ and value IV. Calculate the New price = IV / IQ. These calculations are to be done provided there is no Deletion record. If there is, print an error line D.I.

- If there is no Input with the Old Stock, IV, IQ and the New price are set equal to the value, quantity and price from the Old Stock record.

- If there is no Stock Output, the New Stock quantity = IQ and the New Stock value = IV.

- If there is Stock Output calculate:
    Total Output value = Tot. Out. Qty × price   and then
    New Stock quantity = IQ — Tot. Out. quantity and
    New Stock value   = IV — Tot. Out. value

For a non-deleted product:

- If the difference between Old Price and New Price exceeds 10% of the former, calculate:
    Max. value = Max. × New Price,
    Min. value = Min. × New Price.

- If Old Stock quantity = New Stock quantity and if Old Stock quantity is less than Min. print an error line OS quantity < Min.

- If Old Stock quantity is not equal to New Stock quantity and if New Stock is less than Min., calculate: Re-order quantity = Max. quantity — New Stock quantity even if New-Stock quantity is negative.

- If New Stock quantity is negative print an error line New Stock < 0.

For a deleted product with an Old Stock record and no Input, no output is required.

Do this problem completely correcting your solutions step by step. Start with the Results and Data diagrams.

SOLUTION

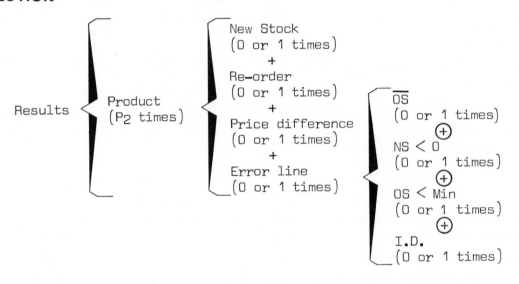

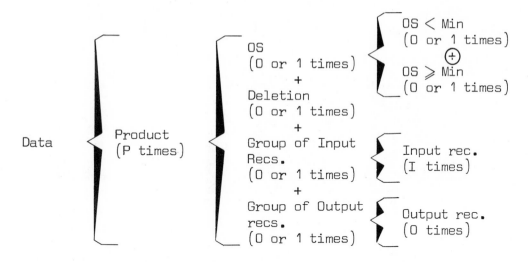

The first processing phase uses the INPUT DATA of the program. This phase includes the following:
- calculate the Total Input quantity and the Total Input value
- calculate the Total Output quantity
- calculate the Intermediate quantity (IQ) and value (IV)
- calculate the New price
- calculate the Total Output value
- calculate the New Stock value and quantity
- delete a product
- detect the error $\overline{OS}$
- detect the error OS quantity $<$ Min if $\overline{I}.\overline{O}.\overline{D}$
- detect the error I.D

The second processing phase includes:
- calculate the Max. value
- calculate the Min. value

The second phase concerns products having an OS record, Input records and no Deletion records.

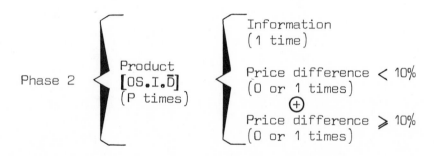

The third phase includes:
- calculate the Re-order quantity
- detect the error NS quantity < 0
- output the New Stock record

This phase concerns products having an OS record and Input or Output records and no Deletion record.

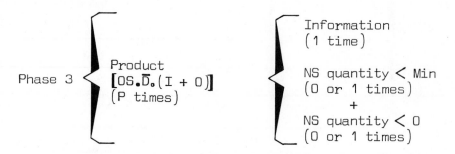

$$\text{Phase 3} \left\{ \begin{array}{l} \text{Product} \\ [\text{OS}.\overline{\text{D}}.(\text{I} + \text{O})] \\ (\text{P times}) \end{array} \right. \left\{ \begin{array}{l} \text{Information} \\ (1\ \text{time}) \\ \\ \text{NS quantity} < \text{Min} \\ (0\ \text{or 1 times}) \\ \qquad + \\ \text{NS quantity} < 0 \\ (0\ \text{or 1 times}) \end{array} \right.$$

Now draw up the truth table for the DATA and prepare the tree structure.

TABLE T1

	φ	1	2	3	4	5	6	7	8	9	10	11	12	13	14	15	16
D	0	0	1	0	1	0	1	0	1	0	1	0	1	0	1	0	1
O	0	0	0	1	1	0	0	1	1	0	0	1	1	0	0	1	1
I	0	0	0	0	0	1	1	1	1	0	0	0	0	1	1	1	1
OS	0	0	0	0	0	0	0	0	0	1	1	1	1	1	1	1	1
① Trans. Phase 2 / Calc. IQ / Calc. IV	φ													×		×	
② Calc. Tot. Output Value	φ															×	
③ Trans. Phase 3	φ											×		×		×	
④ Calc. NS qty. / NS val.	φ									×		×		×		×	
⑤ Test OS qty. < Min.	φ									×							
⑥ Err. I.D	φ														×		×
⑦ Delete	φ										×		×				
⑧ Calc. Tot. Input qty. and value	φ													×	×	×	×
⑨ Calc. Tot. Output qty.	φ											×	×			×	×
⑩ Err. OS	φ	×	×	×	×	×	×	×								

The above table shows that actions ① ② ③ and ⑤ are to be performed on sub-sets for which a New Stock record must be written. Also actions ⑧ ⑨ are to be performed on groups of records which in any case have to be read.

Here is the map for the actions ④ ⑥ ⑦ and ⑩ :

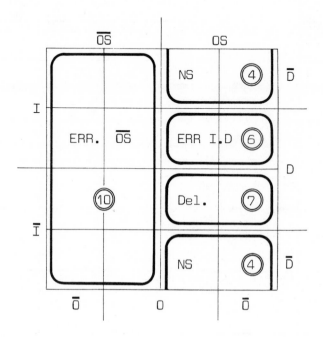

This gives the structure:

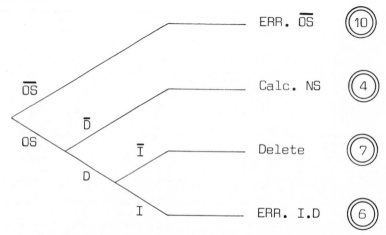

Develop the branch OS.$\bar{D}$ which contains actions ① ② ③ and ⑤ :

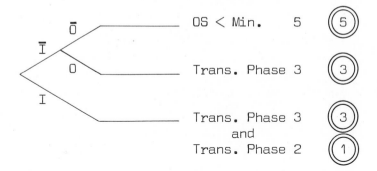

Branch I gives:

The numbering of the actions enables them to be verified thus ensuring that no action is overlooked. Here is the beginning of the decomposition without the determination of the reference criterion:

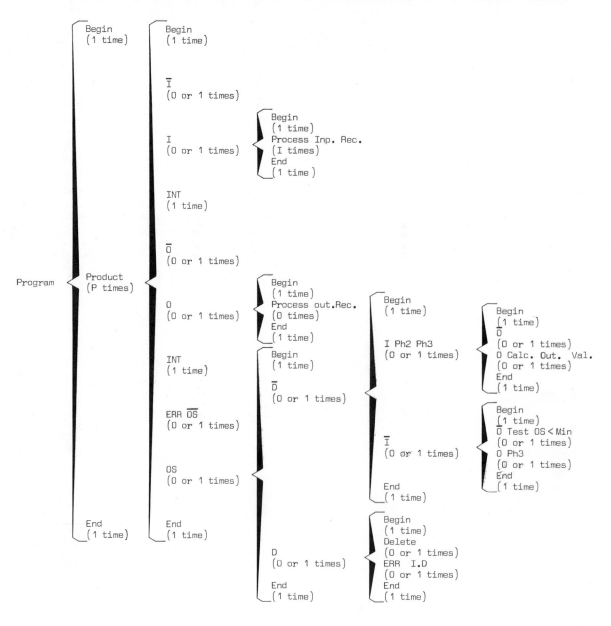

Phase 3 requires a truth table.
Let Y mean NS quantity non-negative
and X mean NS quantity $<$ Min.

X Y	ERR. NS $<$ 0	Write NS	Write Re-order
0 0	φ	φ	φ
0 1		X	
1 0	X		X
1 1		X	X

By using this table and phase 2, the complete decomposition can be done.
The results of Phase 3 must be appended to the 2 branches of the tree already obtained viz.:

   OS.$\bar{\text{D}}$.I
   OS.$\bar{\text{D}}$.$\bar{\text{I}}$.O

Thus a sub-routine (SR NS) is required.
The calculation of the Total Output quantity and value must be done in the branches:

   OS.$\bar{\text{D}}$.I.O
   OS.$\bar{\text{D}}$.$\bar{\text{I}}$.O

Thus a second sub-routine (SR OUT) is required.
To validate the decomposition, the results diagram is reproduced here with each sub-set numbered.
These will be written on the decomposition to ensure that all the results have been obtained.

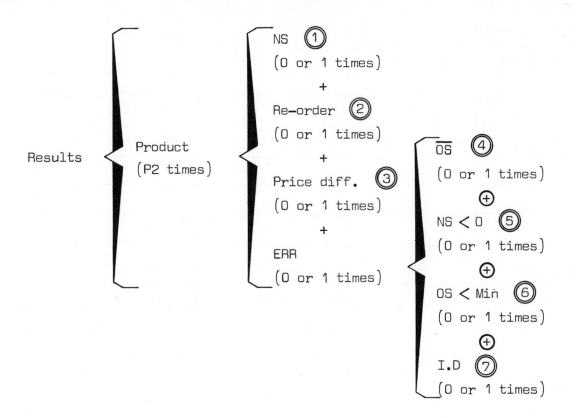

Complete decomposition:

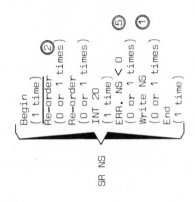

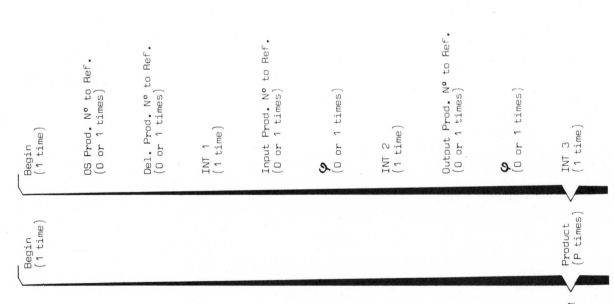

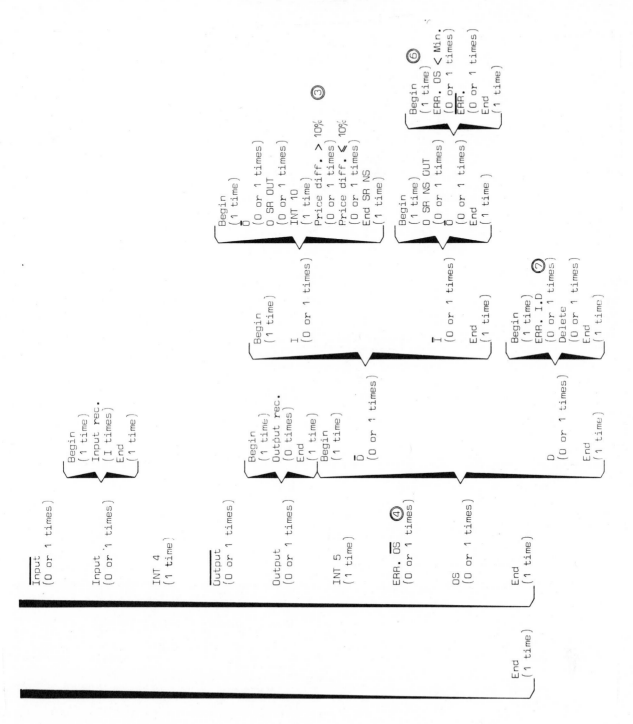

Flowchart:

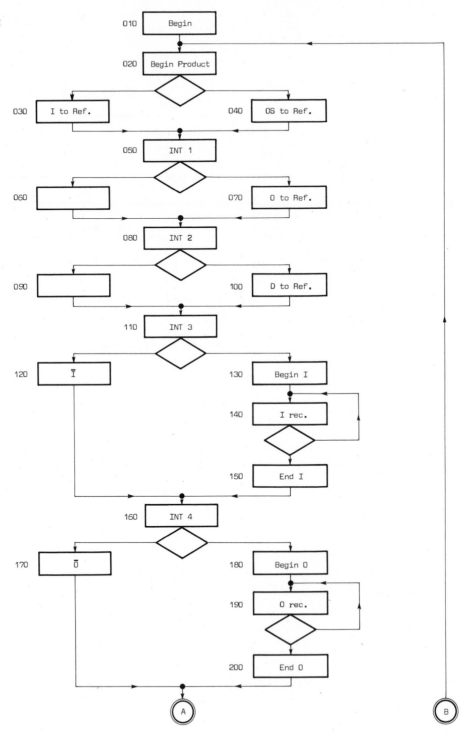

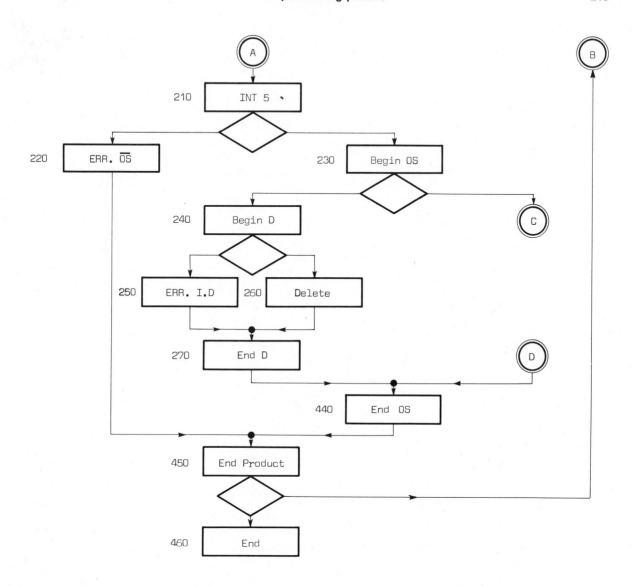

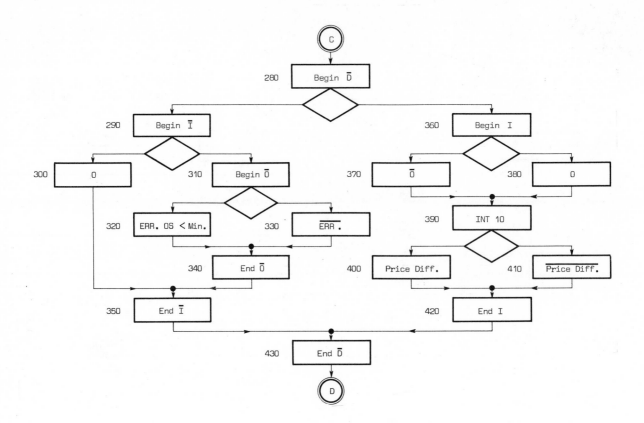

Sub-routines
SR OUT

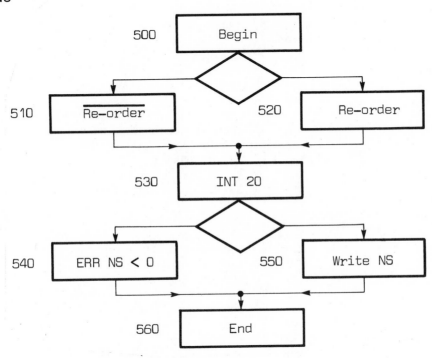

Now do the detailed organisation.

Detailed organisation: Instruction Lists by Type

Read

010 Read 1st OS
010 Read 1st D
010 Read 1st I
010 Read 1st O
440 Read OS
100 Read D
140 Read I
190 Read O

Branch

020 If OS N° < I N°	040
030	050
050 If O N° < Ref	070
060	080
080 If D N° ⩽ Ref	100
090	110
110 If I N° = Ref	130
120	160
140 If I N° = Ref	140
160 If O N° = Ref	180
170	210
190 If O N° = Ref	190
210 If OS N° = Ref	230
220	450
230 If SWD = O	280
240 If SWI = O	260
250	270
270	440
280 If SWI = 1	360
290 If SWO = O	310
300	350
310 If OS Qty ⩾ Min.	330
320	340
350	430
360 If SWO = 1	380
370	390
390 If Price diff ⩽ 10%	410
400	420
450 If $\overline{\text{EOF}}$ (all files)	020
500 If OS Qty < Min.	520
530 If NS ⩾ 0	550
510	530
540	560

Preparation of branch

040 OS N° to Ref
100 D N° to Ref
030 I N° to Ref
070 O N° to Ref
020 Set SWD to 0
020 Set SWI to 0
020 Set SWO to 0
100 Set SWD to 1
130 Set SWI to 1
180 Set SWO to 1

Calculation

130 Clear Tot. Inp. Qty
130 Clear Tot. Inp. value
140 Acc. Inp. Qty
140 Acc. Inp. value
180 Clear Tot. Out. Qty
190 Acc. Out. Qty
280 IQ = OS Qty
280 IV = OS value Inp.
360 IQ = IQ + Tot. Inp. Qty
360 IV = IV + Tot. Inp. value
360 Calc. New price
410 Calc. Min. value
410 Calc. Max. value
520 Calc. Re-Order Qty
600 Calc. Out. value
600 Ns qty = IQ — Tot. Out Qty
600 NS value = IV — Out. value

Output

220 Edit and Print ERR $\overline{\text{OS}}$
250 Edit and Print ERR I.D
320 Edit and Print ERR OS < Min
410 Edit and Write Price Diff. rec.
520 Edit and Write Re-Order rec.
540 Edit and Print ERR NS < 0
550 Edit and Write NS rec.

Sub-routine calls

300 Call SR OUT
380 Call SR OUT
300 Call SR NS
330 Call SR NS
420 Call SR NS

Note that switches are required to avoid records being overlaid.
- SWD in 100
- SWI in 140
- SWO in 190

Note also the way in which D is read: the test at the end of 080 is 'less than or equal to'.
In this way, sequence 100 is executed as many times as there are products deleted. Another possibility would have been to use an alternative structure at the end of the product: If D read another record, if not do nothing.

Detailed organisation: Sorted Instruction List

Sequence	Instruction	Next Sequence
010	Read 1st OS	
	Read 1st D	
	Read 1st I	
	Read 1st O	
020	Set SW D to O	
	Set SW I to O	
	Set SW O to O	
	If OS N° < I N°	040
030	I N° to Ref	050
040	OS N° to Ref	
050	If I N° < Ref	070
060		080
070	O N° to Ref	
080	If D N° ≤ Ref	100
090		110
100	D N° to Ref	
	Set SWD to 1	
	Read D	
110	If I N° = Ref	130
120		160
130	Set SWI to 1	
	Clear Tot. Inp. Qty	
	Clear Tot. Inp. value	
140	Acc. Inp. Qty	
	Acc. Inp. value	
	Read Input	
	If I N° = Ref	140
150		
160	If O N° = Ref	180

170		210
180	Set SWO to 1	
	Clear Tot. Out. Qty	
190	Acc. Out. Qty	
	Read Output	
	If O N° = Ref	190
200		
210	If OS N° = Ref	230
220	Edit and Print ERR $\overline{OS}$	450
230	If SWD = O	280
240	If SWI = O	260
250	Edit and Print ERR I.D	270
260		
270		440
280	IQ = OS Qty	
	IV = OS value	
	If SWI = 1	360
290	If SWO = 0	310
300	Call SR OUT	
	Call SR NS	350
310	If OS Qty $\geqslant$ Min	330
320	Edit and Print ERR OS $<$ Min	340
330	Call SR NS	
340		
350		430
360	IQ = IQ + Tot. Inp. Qty	
	IV = IV + Tot. Inp. value	
	Calculate New Price	
	If SWO = 1	380
370		
380	Cals SR OUT	390
390	If Price diff. $\leqslant$ 10%	410
400		420
410	Calculate Min. value	
	Calculate Max. value	
	Edit and write Price diff. rec.	
420	Call SR NS	
430		
440	Read OS	
450	If $\overline{EOF}$ (All files)	020

Sub-routine SR NS

500	If OS Qty $<$ Min	520	
510		530	
520	Calculate Re-order Qty		
	Edit and Write Re-Order rec.		
530	If NS Qty $\geqslant$ 0	550	
540	Edit and print ERR NS $<$ 0	560	
550	Edit and write NS rec		

Sub-routine SR OUT

600	Calculate Output value
	Calculate NS Qty
	Calculate NS Value

5 — SPECIAL CASES OF COMPLEX ALTERNATING STRUCTURES IN LOGICAL INPUT FILES

Truth tables are not the only tool used in building that part of a program which processes a complex alternating structure in the input data.

When the quantity of data types used 0 or 1 times at the same level of a complex alternating structure is large, there are too many minterms to fit into a single truth table. In such a case, one must use several tables.

If one or more codes are used in the same universal set, and each may have more than three values, it is unpractical to use a single truth table. Here a simple double-entry table is a useful tool in finding the variables necessary to process the structure.

TRUTH TABLES FOR MORE THAN SIX BINARY VARIABLES

When the number of boolean variables in a logical input file's alternating structure exceeds six, a double-entry table is used to identify which data subsets are independent.

Two data subsets, A and B, are independent if none of the variables of A is used as a condition for any action which uses as a condition a variable of B, or vice versa. In other words, if no action is conditioned by variables from both A and B constitute independent subsets.

For each independent subset, a truth table may be built in the usual manner.

Example: taking a subset of the logical input file as universal set R:

A
(0 or 1 times)
        +
B
(0 or 1 times)
        +
C
(0 or 1 times)
        +
DATA
R
D
(0 or 1 times)
        +
E
(0 or 1 times)
        +
F
(0 or 1 times)
        +
G
(0 or 1 times)

Action-conditioning variables are then :

Action 1 = A
Action 2 = A.$\underline{C}$
Action 3 = A.$\overline{C}$.B
Action 4 = D.E
Action 5 = E
Action 6 = $\underline{F}$.G
Action 7 = $\overline{G}$.H

A double-entry table is used to identify the independent variables:

With this table, we find three subsets of independent variables:

R	1	2	3	4	5	6	7
A	X	X	X				
B			X				
C		X	X				
D				X			
E				X	X		
F						X	
G						X	X
H							X

X = {A, B, C} for actions 1, 2, and 3.
Y = {D, E } for actions 4 and 5.
Z = {F, G, H } for actions 6, and 7.

The result is a group of three truth tables, which yield the required program subset:

X A B C	1	2	3
0 0 0			
0 0 1			
0 1 0			
0 1 1			
1 0 0	X		
1 0 1	X	X	
1 1 0	X		X
1 1 1	X	X	

Y D E	4	5
0 0		
0 1		
1 0		X
1 1	X	X

Z	6	7
0 0 0		
0 0 1		X
0 1 0		
0 1 1		
1 0 0		
1 0 1		X
1 1 0	X	
1 1 1	X	

```
PROGRAM
(Universal)

  Begin R
  (0 or 1 times)

  A
  (0 or 1 times)

  Ā
  (0 or 1 times)

  Intermediate 1
  (1 time)

  D
  (0 or 1 times)

  D̄
  (0 or 1 times)

  Intermediate 2
  (1 times)

  F
  (0 or 1 times)

  F̄
  (0 or 1 times)

  Intermediate 3
  (1 time)

  H
  (0 or 1 times)

  H̄
  (0 or 1 times)

  End R
  (1 time)

    Begin A - Action
    (1 time)

    C - Action 2
    (0 or 1 times)

    C̄
    (0 or 1 times)

    End A
    (1 time)

      Begin C̄
      (1 time)

      B    action 3
      (0 or 1 times)

      B̄
      (0 or 1 times)

      End
      (1 time)

    Begin D - Action 5
    (1 time)

    E - Action 4
    (0 or 1 times)

    Ē
    (0 or 1 times)

    End D
    (1 time)

    Begin F
    (1 time)

    G - Action 6
    (0 or 1 times)

    Ḡ
    (0 or 1 times)

    End F
    (1 time)

    Begin H
    (1 time)

    G
    (0 or 1 times)

    Ḡ - Action 7
    (0 or 1 times)

    End H
    (1 time)
```

If a single table of eight boolean variables had been used, the number of minterms required would have been $2^8 = 256$. Using the three tables instead reduces the number of minterms to $8 + 4 + 8 = 20$.

CODES HAVING MORE THAN THREE VALUES

When a code has more than three possible values, it is useful to build a tee-structured program, using a truth table to determine the sequence of tests performed in the program.

Example: taking a code with three possible values, any other values being treated as error conditions, we can describe the code:

$$\text{Data} \left\{ \text{Code} \left[= 1, = 2, = 3, = \text{others}, 0 \text{ or } 1 \text{ times} \right] \right.$$

The actions to be taken are:

Action a if code = 1
Action b if code = 1 or 2
Action c if code = 3

with an error message for any other value.

The resulting truth table:

	a	b	c	ERR
1	X	X		
2		X		
3			X	
Others				X

and the resulting program:

$$\text{PROGRAM} \left\{ \begin{array}{l} \text{Start} \\ (1 \text{ time}) \\ \\ \text{Code} \left[= 1, 0\text{--}1 \text{ times} \right] \\ \text{Subroutine b Action a} \\ \\ \text{Code} \left[= \overline{1}, 0\text{--}1 \text{ times} \right] \\ \\ \text{End} \\ (1 \text{ time}) \end{array} \right.$$

$$\left\{ \begin{array}{l} \text{Start} \\ (1 \text{ time}) \\ \\ \text{Code} \left[= 2, 0\text{--}1 \text{ times} \right] \\ \text{Subroutine b} \\ \text{Code} \left[= \overline{2}, 0\text{--}1 \text{ times} \right] \\ \\ \text{End} \\ (1 \text{ time}) \end{array} \right.$$

$$\left\{ \begin{array}{l} \text{Start} \\ (1 \text{ time}) \\ \\ \text{Code} \left[= 3, 0\text{--}1 \text{ times} \right] \\ \text{Action C} \\ \\ \text{Code} \left[= \overline{3}, 0\text{--}1 \text{ times} \right] \\ \text{ERR} \\ \\ \text{End} \\ (1 \text{ time}) \end{array} \right.$$

SEVERAL CODES WITH MORE THAN TWO VALUES EACH

When a number of codes, each with more than two possible values, is used at the same level of logical input file, a decision table is needed to construct the program.

Example: in the subset R of the logical input file, two codes are used:

$$\text{Data}\atop\text{R} \begin{cases} \text{Code } x \left[= 1, \ = 2, \ = \text{others values}, \ 0 \text{ or } 1 \text{ times} \right] \\ \text{Code } y \left[= 1, \ = 2, \ = 3, \ = \text{others values}, \ 0 \text{ or } 1 \text{ times} \right] \end{cases}$$

The actions to be taken are:

Action a if (code x = 1) . (code y = 2)

Action b if (code x = 2) . (code y = 3)

Action c if (code y = 2).

Error x for any other value of code x.

Error y for any other value of code y.

The resulting truth table:

R	a	b	c	ERR x	ERR y
x = 1	X				
x = 2		X			
x = others				X	
y = 1	X				
y = 2			X		
y = 3		X			
y = others					X

and one of the possible resulting program subsets:

PROGRAM
(Universal)

Begin
(1 time)

Process if x = 1
(0 or 1 times)

Begin
(1 time)

Process if y = 1 → action a
(0 or 1 times)

Process if $\overline{y = 1}$
(0 or 1 times)

End
(1 time)

Process if $\overline{x = 1}$
(0 or 1 times)

INTERMEDIATE
(1 time)

Begin
(1 time)

Process if x = 2
(0 or 1 times)

Process if $\overline{x = 2}$
(0 or 1 times)

End
(1 time)

Begin
(1 time)
Process if y = 3 → action b
(0 or 1 times)
Process if $\overline{y = 3}$
(0 or 1 times)
End
(1 time)

"ERROR"
SUBROUTINE

Process if → action c
y = 2
(0 or 1 times)

Process if $\overline{y = 2}$
(0 or 1 times)

End
(1 time)

Begin
(1 time)

Process if y = 1
(0 or 1 times)

Process if $\overline{y = 1}$
(0 or 1 times)

End
(1 time)

Begin
(1 time)
Process if y = 3
(0 or 1 times)
Process if $\overline{y = 3}$
(0 or 1 times)
End
(1 time)

"ERROR"
SUBROUTINE

INDEX